The
BRIDE'S MONEY BOOK

The BRIDE'S MONEY BOOK

How to Have a Champagne Wedding *on a Ginger-Ale Budget*

Pamela A. Piljac
author of *The Bride's Thank-You Guide* and
The Bride-To-Bride Book

CHICAGO REVIEW PRESS

Library of Congress Cataloging-in-Publication Data

Piljac, Pamela A., 1954–
 The bride's money book : how to have a champagne wedding on a ginger-ale budget / by Pamela A. Piljac. — 1st ed.
   p.   cm.
  ISBN 1-55652-261-4
  1. Weddings—Planning. 2. Wedding etiquette. I. Title.
 HQ745.P54 1996
 395'.22—dc20   95-25464
                                                                                CIP

© 1996 by Pamela A. Piljac
All rights reserved

First edition
Published by Chicago Review Press, Incorporated
814 North Franklin Street
Chicago, Illinois 60610
ISBN 1-55652-261-4

5 4 3 2 1

For Rick Linn
who shouldn't remain unacknowledged

Contents

Preface ix

Introduction xi

Part One   **Making A Plan**   1

   From One Bride to Another 3

   Weddings: An Overview 4

   Wedding Costs: What to Expect 5

   Who Pays for What? 10

   Setting Priorities 13

   Examining Your Budget 16

   Relying on Monetary Gifts 23

   Keeping to a Realistic Budget 24

   Using the Record and Accounting Diary Worksheets 24

   Why Get Organized? 46

   The Best Way to Organize 47

   Wedding Consultants: Are They Worth the Expense? 50

   Service Providers: Getting the Most for Your Money 52

Part Two   **Sample Weddings**   63

   A Formal Church Ceremony and Reception 65

   A Ceremony and Reception at Home 66

   A Garden Ceremony and Reception 68

   A Hotel Ceremony and Reception 69

A Ceremony at City Hall and an Intimate Dinner Reception at a Restaurant 71

A Small Informal Civil Ceremony and Cake-Cutting Reception on a Boat 72

A Formal Church Ceremony and a Small Dinner Reception at a Hotel 73

A Formal Church Ceremony and a Large Dinner Reception at a Mansion 75

Last-Minute Planning: An Informal Wedding 76

Last-Minute Planning: A Formal Wedding 77

Part Three Money-Saving Ideas 81

Accessories 83	Headpiece 93
Attendants 83	Honeymoon 93
Beverages 84	Invitations 94
Cake 85	Music 95
Catering 86	Photography and Videography 95
Ceremony Site 87	Reception Site 96
Decorations 87	Rings 97
Flowers 87	Service Providers 97
Food 89	Setting the Date 98
Formal Attire 90	Transportation 98
Gown 90	Two Things You Should Not Do to Save Money 98
Guest List 92	

Preface

You would like to plan an unforgettable wedding day and bring to life the day of your dreams. If you're like most of us, you want your wedding to include beautiful flowers, excellent food and music, cheerful attendants, a breathtaking gown, an adoring spouse, and friends and family sharing the festivities.

In your dreams, this may be a quiet, refined affair in an elegant setting. In your best friend's fantasies, it may be an elaborate production with two live bands and everyone she's ever met in attendance.

Have you thought about who you want to be on your wedding day? Every bride's imagination casts her in a special role—the fairy princess, majestic queen, country maid, medieval wench, Victorian lady, captivating enchantress, or elegant sophisticate. It's time to make your dreams come true.

A marriage celebration is a timeless ingredient in nearly every social tradition. In the past, a wedding might represent the combining of two family properties or a bond in a political alliance. Today, two people promise to work together, to take care of each other's needs, and to share hopes, dreams, and decisions. Traditionally, the climax of the event is a merry gathering packed with festivities for all to enjoy.

Marriage is a momentous occasion. And pledging to work side by side as a couple has more meaning today because we live longer than previous generations. It only makes sense that you'd want to start off this major commitment with a rollicking good time. We'll create yours together.

Most large family gatherings occur at weddings and funerals. When you make your plans, stop and imagine for a moment that you are a guest at the wedding. For your relatives, that day will be their time to visit with far-flung relatives they may not see again. It might be the first time they meet all of the members of your extended families. Have a party for your wedding that everyone will enjoy. I'm not suggesting that you ignore your own preferences, just take other people's into consideration.

A wedding is more than making a commitment or having a romantic day with beautiful gowns and flowers and music. It is the fulfillment of centuries-old customs and traditions that have been practiced in so many cultures because they satisfy a deep social need.

You wouldn't be reading this book if you didn't recognize that. Now it is time for you to begin creating the celebration for the gathering of both your families.

Introduction

Throughout this book you'll follow Rachel and Mark as they work through the process of planning their wedding. I'll then describe their wedding day in detail, and their feelings and insights afterward. I'll share the stories and suggestions of many other couples, too. Here you'll find straightforward wedding anecdotes. You'll learn to use worksheets and questionnaires to help you create a delightful and memorable day. You'll discover how to set priorities, get organized, and keep costs down.

This isn't a wedding planner. I won't tell you when to order invitations, or how to word them. I already wrote the ideal book to help with planning, etiquette, and making decisions about all the details. It's called *The Bride to Bride Book*. Ask for it at your local bookstore.

This book will help you find ways to pay for your plans. You'll discover practical ideas and suggestions that will help you keep spending under control by keeping your costs down and setting a realistic budget. In addition, there are more than 235 specific and practical money-saving ideas covering all wedding-related categories, from rings to the honeymoon.

To give you an overview of what to expect I'll begin with advice from a recent bride. Turn the page for a helpful letter written by Rachel's cousin Ashley, shortly after Rachel and Mark became engaged.

Part One

MAKING A PLAN

From One Bride to Another

Dear Rachel,

Congratulations! Eric and I are so happy for you and Mark, and we know you will have a beautiful life together. I can't wait for your wedding and wish that I didn't live 3,000 miles away, because I would like to help you plan it all. But I'll do the best I can, and I hope this letter will help.

It's funny. For an entire year, my whole life was consumed with planning my wedding. Now that we've been married fifteen months it is all a wonderful but blurred memory.

We spent a lot of time talking about the kind of wedding we wanted and what we liked about other weddings we attended. We both agreed that we didn't want to go into debt. Our first goal was to learn how much my parents could contribute and how much we could save from our own paychecks. Then we would know how much the wedding could cost.

We had a lot of temptations. It wasn't easy, but we did manage to stay close to that budget. It's a special time when you are trying to create a perfect dream day, and there are so many beautiful things to choose—sometimes things can get out of hand.

At one point I almost called the whole thing off. Eric insisted we couldn't afford the reception at Beaumont Hills. That's where I always wanted to have my wedding, and I couldn't believe he was so insensitive to my dream! Then he found the Alabar, which was two-and-a-half times less expensive than Beaumont Hills—and an equally gorgeous setting.

That is the key to making it work: finding alternatives, compromising, or giving up one item so that you can have another.

For Eric, it was important that we have two live bands, one jazz, one rock, at the reception. He worked very hard, calling everyone in the directory and driving all over trying to find good, affordable musicians to make it work. He couldn't put it together. He did arrange to have an hour of live jazz played by a trio. And we had a good deejay for the rest of the night.

Spend the time and make the effort to learn what you want. Then determine if you can afford to pay the price, or if there is a way to have something similar that is less expensive.

I also think that deep down too many of us have a silly superstition that for our married life to be perfect, we must have an ideal wedding day. That presumption puts an enormous amount of pressure on every decision you make. And it's definitely not true. If you don't believe me, sit down with Grandma and Aunt Beverly sometime and listen to the disasters that happened at their weddings. And they've been married forty and fifty years!

Another unrealistic expectation I had was that I would "know" when I tried on the perfect wedding gown. I think that only happens in movies. I love the dress I bought, and it was the third one I tried on. Since I didn't feel magically enchanted when I looked in the mirror, I spent four more Saturdays going to every store within fifty miles to try on dresses. It was an incredible waste of my time. If you find a dress you like that is comfortable and you can afford it—buy it!

On my wedding day I woke up incredibly nervous, and worried myself sick over countless details that could go wrong. If I can help you in any way it would be to tell you to relax and enjoy your day. It passes very quickly, and chances are something will go wrong whether you worry or not. I bet you never noticed at my wedding that the caterers forgot to bring the crab appetizers. Or that the centerpieces the florist delivered to the reception hall featured the wrong colors. To me, it was a disaster, and I let it spoil my celebration.

Eric refused to pay either of them until they reduced their bills to compensate for their errors. I learned afterward that no one else even noticed.

The real irony is that my mom and I argued for weeks over the color of the reception flowers. In the end, neither of us had what we wanted. And that is my last piece of advice, Rachel. Listen to everyone's suggestions and ideas, but please yourself and Mark. It's your day. I hope it will be a happy and joyful one!

Best wishes and lots of love,

Ashley

Weddings: An Overview

Rachel asked Mark to read Ashley's letter. They talked about her suggestions and decided to make a general list of everything that would be involved in planning the wedding.

Mark said, "It seems the first thing we need to decide is the date."

"From what I've heard," Rachel said, "some of the best locations and service providers are booked months, even years in advance. So first we have to get an idea of the dates these places are available. We need to establish what kind of wedding we want, where the ceremony will be, and what music, readings, vows, and rituals we want for the ceremony. We also need to decide where we would like to hold the reception and how much it will cost."

"I want John to be my best man," Mark said.

"I've already asked Annie to be my maid of honor."

After a brief argument over the size of the wedding party, the couple agreed they each would have four attendants, in addition to two ushers. Rachel would contact both sets of parents for their guest list suggestions. She began listing the service providers they would need, including the caterer, photographer, videographer, musicians, florist, baker, and chauffeur.

"We need to decide what items we want them to provide, and then sign a contract with them. I'll also need to select my gown and headpiece, and clothing for my attendants. And you'll need to choose the apparel you and the male members of the wedding party will wear."

"We need to find our rings," Mark said, "and learn what requirements and tests are required to obtain our marriage license."

"We also need to select and order our invitations, announcements, and thank-you note stationery," said Rachel, "and purchase gifts for the attendants. But first we need a better idea of what kind of wedding we want to have, and how much it will cost. If we can't afford what we want, let's find out early in the process, before we really have our hearts set on a particular item or specific place."

Wedding Costs: What to Expect

The next Saturday the couple sat down with tablets, pens, calculators, and both sets of parents.

"Your first step is to decide what kind of wedding you are having. Then you can obtain estimates to see if that is what you can afford," Rachel's mom told them. "Your father and I can contribute $4,500 toward the wedding expenses," she added. "We wish it could be more, but it is yours to spend as you please."

"We want you to have a keepsake of your wonderful memories and would like to pay for the photography and videography." Mark's mom said. "However, please keep that expense under $1,000."

Rachel and Mark thanked their parents. Since they had planned to pay for most of the wedding themselves, their parents' contributions would certainly help. However, they still weren't sure how much money they needed, or how much they would each be able to contribute.

After studying a wedding planner and etiquette book, Rachel told Mark, "It seems like there are four basic wedding styles."

"Very formal is the traditional, elaborate wedding with elegant attire, a huge guest list, lavish food, lots of musicians—the kind of high-society wedding we often see in movies.

"Formal, the most popular and well-known style of wedding, doesn't follow the strictest rules of etiquette that the very formal wedding does, but still conforms to custom and protocol. The bride and her attendants still wear long gowns, and the groom and his attendants dress in formal attire. But the number of attendants, size of the guest list, and elaboration and expense of everything else is less. And by the way, what we wear if we have a very formal or formal wedding is also determined by the time of day."

"What do you mean?" asked Mark.

Rachel flipped through the pages. "Well, if we have a formal daytime wedding, it says you would wear a tuxedo or stroller in the traditional colors of black or gray—unless we marry between May and September, then you can wear white. If we have the same style of wedding but marry in the evening, you can wear a tuxedo or a formal dinner jacket."

"I've always liked the idea of a tailcoat. What kind of wedding do we need to have for that?"

"That would be a very formal evening wedding," replied Rachel. "During the day you can wear a long jacket, stroller, or cutaway coat for this style of wedding.

"Now semiformal and informal weddings are a lot more flexible. That would be anything from me in a dress and you in a suit to us saying our vows before we jump out of an airplane."

After discussing different kinds of weddings, the couple concluded that even if they planned a simple civil ceremony at a justice of the peace, they would still have to pay for:

Attire

Ceremony officiant

Flowers

Licenses

Medical tests

Rings

And any other wedding style, no matter how simple, would still include the expenses of:

- Ceremony site
- Entertainment (optional)
- Photography
- Reception
- Refreshments

As Rachel and Mark quickly learned, it's not which items or activities you include in your day, but how grand and expensive you permit them to be. And the golden rule is *the larger the wedding, the more elaborate the festivities, the bigger the bills.*

A formal wedding can start at $4,500 and run to $30,000, or more. If you plan your wedding to fit your budget, it will cost what you can afford.

Where to marry, what to wear, the number of guests, and the size and type of reception can vary immensely. It is very difficult to be specific about costs, because an identical dress or caterer in New York City might cost three times more than it does in Butte, Montana. Some say that an average formal wedding with 200 guests now costs about $16,000. That price tag might be enough to scare you away, but it's not necessarily true for your wedding.

First, that's an average. It accounts for expensive, elaborate celebrations, as well as simple, informal affairs. In addition, the surveys often include items you will not personally pay for—such as attire for male and female attendants—or may not consider part of the wedding celebration costs—such as engagement and wedding rings. Lastly, these surveys are often done among wedding consultants. And people seldom use wedding consultants unless they are having a larger, more expensive wedding.

You'll later learn how Rachel and Mark used a combination of sources to come up with an average cost breakdown. Their information was based on a formal wedding and reception with a sit-down meal for 200 guests. Here is what they discovered.

Their food budget was for a sit-down dinner that included roast beef, fried chicken, vegetable lasagna, mashed potatoes, garden and pasta salads, two vegetable side dishes, bread and rolls, coffee, and tea. The price was based on $21 a plate.

Beverages, including beer, wine, simple mixed drinks, and soda pop, were budgeted at $525. They realized that a nonalcoholic reception would be a lot less expensive, but decided to serve some alcoholic beverages anyway.

They allowed a $400 rental charge for the reception site. In some cases the rental charge was much less, but they would be required to use on-site catering at a higher per plate charge.

Their music budget of $850 left two options: $350 for musicians and vocalists at the ceremony, and $500 for a deejay at the reception; or $850 for a live, five-piece band performing for four hours at the wedding reception.

An $800 budget for the gown and headpiece was based on an average of several ensembles found in a nearby bridal shop. They were not designer gowns of overly expensive materials or with elaborate decoration—just lovely garments of good quality and attractive design.

An estimate of $700 for the photography was based on a minimal package of still photos covering the wedding ceremony and reception only. They decided not to include an engagement portrait, or photos of the bride at home preparing for the ceremony, because it would mean adding $250.

The cost of a video album of their wedding day would depend on the number of cameras used, length of the video, number of locations, and skill and reputation of the videographer. Their budget of $300 was based on an average of quotes obtained for videotaping both the wedding and reception.

They learned that the key to keeping the floral budget in line is avoiding costly flowers such as orchids and gardenias, and selecting flowers that are in season during the wedding. Their budget of $617 includes:

> four corsages at $8 each (for mothers and grandmothers)
>
> ten boutonnieres at $5 each (for four male attendants, two ushers, both fathers, and two grandfathers)
>
> four bouquets for female attendants at $45 each
>
> one groom's boutonniere at $10
>
> one bridal bouquet at $65
>
> four church baskets at $45 each
>
> reception centerpieces and arrangements at $100

A $580 budget for tips, fees, attendants' gifts, and miscellaneous items seemed high at first, but estimated expenses added up quickly. They included $130 to the ceremony officiant, $100 for medical tests, and $50 for the marriage license. They would each have four attendants, plus two ushers, which totaled to ten gifts at about $20 each. That left $100 for miscellaneous gratuities.

The stationery budget of $500 was based on a simple, traditional formal invitation with response cards and return envelopes, a basic thank-you note, and 450 postage stamps (for a 150-invitation mailing, thank-you note mailing, plus postage on the response card).

Estimates of $240 for the wedding cake were based on the number of servings. Their budget was for an attractively decorated layer cake and a medium-priced cake-top decoration.

They learned that some limousine services charge by the hour, others for the entire day. A basic estimate for service to the ceremony and reception, plus tip, would be approximately $180.

Here is a summary of Rachel and Mark's estimated costs for a wedding and reception with a meal for 200 guests:

Dinner at $21 per plate	$4,200
Beverages	$525
Site Rental	$400
Music	$850
Gown and headpiece	$800
Formal attire rental (groom)	$150
Photography	$700
Videography	$300
Flowers	$617
Fees, gifts, tips, and miscellaneous	$580
Invitations, stationery, and postage	$500
Cake	$240
Transportation	$180
Total	**$10,042**

Rachel and Mark already knew that they would have a combined contribution of $5,500 from their parents toward the expenses. That meant they needed to contribute approximately $4,550 to have the wedding they wanted. As an older independent couple, they expected to pay a significant portion of their own wedding costs. But let's take a moment to discuss the customary breakdown of wedding expenses.

Who Pays for What?

Traditionally, the bride's parents paid for the entire cost of the wedding and reception. Today, many families have flexible arrangements for covering these costs. Many couples pay for the entire affair themselves. Or they may fund it through a combination of contributors from both their families, which might include: the bride's and groom's parents, grandparents, aunts, uncles, and even siblings. However, these unconventional contributions should be entirely voluntary—you must wait for the giver to offer. And you shouldn't accept more than you know they can afford to give.

There are a variety of ways to split the expenses:

Traditional Breakdown

The bride pays for the groom's ring, a gift to the groom, gifts to the bridesmaids, a bridesmaids' luncheon, accommodations for her out-of-town attendants, her physical exam (optional), and any of her required blood and medical tests.

The groom pays for the bride's engagement and wedding rings, a gift to the bride, his attire, gifts for his ushers and best man, the bridal bouquet, boutonnieres for his attendants, corsages for the mothers and selected relatives, his physical exam, the marriage license, any of his required blood and medical tests, accommodations for his out-of-town attendants, the officiant's fee, and the honeymoon trip.

The bride's family pays for the wedding announcements and invitations, the bride's dress and accessories, the bride's trousseau, all photography and videography, bouquets for the bridesmaids, floral arrangements for the ceremony and reception, the rental fee for the ceremony site, security and parking attendants, all the food, liquor and other beverages for the reception, the musicians for the ceremony and reception, and transportation for the bridal party to both the ceremony and reception.

The groom's family pays their own travel expenses and accommodations (if they are from out of town), the rehearsal dinner (if one is held), the wedding breakfast (if one is held—and it is not the reception).

The wedding attendants (bridesmaids, groomsmen, ushers, the best man, the maid or matron of honor) pay for their wedding attire, any travel costs if they are from out of town, and their wedding gift. It is also customary for female attendants to participate in organizing the wedding-related showers.

Some popular untraditional methods of financing:

A Portion for Each

Divide the total cost of the wedding three ways. You and your fiancé pay a third, your parents pay a third, and your fiancé's parents pay a third.

It's in the Bank

Your parents, his parents, and other relatives (such as grandparents) each pledge to contribute a specified amount. The funds are placed in a bank account opened only for wedding expenses. Your budget is based on those pledges, and anything additional you and your fiancé are sure you can contribute.

Long Division

Each family or contributor divides individual wedding categories. For example, you pay for your own gown, headpiece, accessories, and the cake; your mom pays for all the flowers, invitations, and stationery; and your dad pays for the photography, videography, and transportation. Your fiancé pays for the ceremony expenses, reception music, and beverages, and his parents offer to pay the entire catering bill.

Divide the Day

You, and/or your parents, pay all the ceremony-related expenses. Reception costs are divided among the groom's family and any other contributors.

If you are considering nontraditional financial arrangements, it must be handled with extreme tact and diplomacy. In some families, the mere suggestion of varying from the traditional financers would be met with outrage or insult. In others, relatives are delighted to offer their assistance.

If you want your fiancé's family to help, he should first approach them, on his own. Your presence would make this discussion very awkward. Remember, his family is not obligated to help, even if they have lots of money. And your parents shouldn't be asked to put on a celebration beyond their financial ability.

When assistance is offered to you, try to make things as specific as possible to avoid confusion later. For example:

Aunt Martha takes you aside and offers to "do her part" to help make your day as special as possible. Find out exactly what she means. Since Aunt Martha is financially very well-off, you might assume that she's offering to pay a considerable portion for the wedding. You gleefully go out and spend much more than you can afford. Later you discover she meant she would gladly allow out-of-town guests to sleep in her mansion.

Imagine six or more people planning a large and expensive venture; then throw in all the emotions that a wedding can generate. You can be sure there will be hurt feelings, disagreements, and a frustrated bride and groom.

You and your mother might argue over where to hold the ceremony—the family church or a local park. Your dad might want you to hire cousin Karl's oompah band, while your future mother-in-law insists on a formal string quartet. Your grandfather has offered to pay half the catering bill, but only if you serve beef—and you're both vegetarian. His grandmother wants her lifelong friend to make the wedding cake—and for it to be a surprise. Your fiancé hates the traditional white cake and wants a tower of chocolate.

Control over the wedding plans is generally apportioned based on tradition, not on the amount of money one contributes. Customarily, the bride and groom, and then the bride's parents have the greatest say in the decisions. (Unless the groom's family is paying for the entire affair, in which case they are considered the hosts.)

It's a good idea to sit down with everyone who will contribute financially and discuss the general plans. If your parents can't afford the wedding you want, you'll have to contribute the difference, or pare down your plans. If money isn't the problem, just remember that compromises are essential and disagreements are inevitable. It never hurts to *listen* to ideas and suggestions. However, you both should feel comfortable at your ceremony and reception.

If monetary contributions come with strings attached, it may be best to plan a wedding you can afford on your own.

These are three other important things to keep in mind:

- Long-term family relationships are more important than winning little squabbles.
- Be very clear and specific about who will pay what bills and when they will pay them.
- It's best for one person, such as yourself, to oversee everything.

Although it's not required by etiquette, if his parents contribute to the cost of the wedding (beyond their traditional portions) it's a nice touch to include their names along with yours on the invitations. For suggestions, see *The Bride to Bride Book* for wording your invitations.

Setting Priorities

What do you care about the most? The least? What is your fiancé's major interest? Some people think that good food is an essential component for a celebration. To others, the best music, a big crowd, or the nicest location is more significant. Together you have to set your priorities before you can make a realistic budget.

Take a moment and think about weddings you've attended. What features did you enjoy? What would you most miss if it were eliminated? The ceremony and reception are two events that tie the day together, and each will have items you'll want to incorporate, such as special songs, flowers, and rituals.

Do you imagine getting married in front of a small group in a tiny chapel? In an exotic setting? Do you imagine the party afterward as a small, intimate affair? Or a large, festive celebration?

What kind of compromises are you willing to make to have what you want? I will go into more detail later, but here is a simple example that may help now.

Problem:
Food, especially a sit-down dinner with a varied menu, is the biggest expense in most wedding receptions. You want to have a grand-scale party, with lots of friends and live music, but you can't afford the big catering bill.

Solution:
You don't have to have a meal. You can start the reception later in the evening, and have snacks and beverages available for your guests.

Take some time to decide what is most important to you. That is where you will want to focus your expenditures. There are twelve items listed below.

Number them based on their significance to you, (one highest twelve the lowest). Use a pencil since you may change your mind a few times. There is also a Groom's Priority List so that your fiancé can do the same.

Bride's Priority List

__ Ceremony site
__ Catering
__ Gown and headpiece
__ Photography
__ Beverages
__ Videography

__ Reception site
__ Music
__ Flowers
__ Invitations
__ Cake
__ Transportation

Groom's Priority List

__ Ceremony site
__ Catering
__ Formal attire
__ Photography
__ Beverages
__ Videography

__ Reception site
__ Music
__ Flowers
__ Invitations
__ Cake
__ Transportation

Now compare the two. This is where you learn to compromise. Here is how Rachel and Mark recorded their priorities:

Rachel's Priority List

<u>1</u> Ceremony site
<u>9</u> Catering
<u>4</u> Gown and headpiece
<u>5</u> Photography
<u>11</u> Beverages
<u>6</u> Videography

<u>2</u> Reception site
<u>3</u> Music
<u>7</u> Flowers
<u>8</u> Invitations
<u>10</u> Cake
<u>12</u> Transportation

Mark's Priority List

<u>12</u>	Ceremony site	<u>3</u>	Reception site
<u>2</u>	Catering	<u>1</u>	Music
<u>7</u>	Formal attire	<u>10</u>	Flowers
<u>4</u>	Photographs	<u>11</u>	Invitations
<u>6</u>	Beverages	<u>8</u>	Cake
<u>5</u>	Videography	<u>9</u>	Transportation

Before you make major concessions, examine the list below. You don't want to start skimping on items that are actually a small portion of the wedding costs unless you really have to. Here are the percentages of what is spent on each item at a typical formal wedding with 200 guests and a sit-down dinner:

Food, beverages, reception site	53%
Music	9%
Gown and headpiece	8%
Photography	7%
Flowers	6%
Stationery and postage	5%
Fees, gifts, miscellaneous	3%
Videography	3%
Cake	2%
Transportation	2%
Ceremony site	1%
Formal attire	1%

Once you decide where you want to concentrate your expenditures, you can budget the rest. It makes sense to cut costs in the most expensive areas first. Saving 10 percent of the cost of a $300 cake is fairly insignificant. But saving 10 percent of your $6,000 catering bill will make an enormous difference in your total costs.

To stay within your budget you must maintain records of your estimates, as well as the amount you actually spend. The following worksheets allow you to keep a running tally, and continually track whether you are above or below your budgeted amount for each item. This is the best way to fine-tune your planning and keep expenses in line.

Examining Your Budget

Rachel and Mark sat down and took some time to work through the numbers. They needed to know exactly how much they could each contribute. First, they looked at a few recent paycheck stubs and determined their average net monthly after-tax income.

Rachel's after-tax income	$3,100
Mark's after-tax income	$3,850

List your own amounts below:

Bride's monthly after-tax income	_____
Groom's monthly after-tax income	_____

The couple then looked through their checkbooks, bills, receipts, and anything else that would help them determine their average expenses for each month.

As you do your calculations, it is important that you write them down. Be realistic. The wonderful thing about numbers is that you can do anything with them on paper. So don't put down $300 a month for food if you really spend $600. This is not a time for wishful thinking; you need to know exactly what you have to work with. Think of the anxiety you will feel if you underestimate your expenses and commit to spending more than you really can afford. Your goal is a happy, stress-free wedding day. Start making it that way right now by being realistic in everything you do.

If you and your fiancé plan to pay for some or all of the wedding costs together, it is important that you each examine your current assets and expenses now, and determine what you can afford. Set up a special bank account or money market fund for your wedding. Be sure to keep the money separate from all other accounts.

Bride's Current Monthly Living Expenses

Food _____

Rent _____

Utilities _____

Water _____

Telephone _____

Transportation _____

Clothing _____

Hair care _____

Hobbies _____

Dry cleaning _____

Laundry _____

Pets _____

Home decorating _____

Books and magazines _____

Gifts _____

Church and charities _____

Entertainment _____

Life insurance _____

Car insurance _____

Other insurance _____

Medical bills _____

Car payment _____

Credit card debts _____

Other loans/debts _____

Savings and retirement _____

Total _____

Groom's Current Monthly Living Expenses

Food _____

Rent _____

Utilities _____

Water _____

Telephone _____

Transportation _____

Clothing _____

Hair care _____

Hobbies _____

Dry cleaning _____

Laundry _____

Pets _____

Home decorating _____

Books and magazines _____

Gifts _____

Church and charities _____

Entertainment _____

Life insurance _____

Car insurance _____

Other insurance _____

Medical bills _____

Car payment _____

Credit card debts _____

Other loans/debts _____

Savings and retirement _____

Total _____

Rachel's Current Monthly Living Expenses

Food	$400
Rent	$850
Utilities	$200
Water	$65
Telephone	$75
Transportation	$40
Clothing	$200
Hair care	$70
Hobbies	$50
Dry cleaning	$25
Laundry	$40
Pets	$20
Home decorating	$30
Books and magazines	$30
Gifts	$25
Church and charities	$20
Entertainment	$40
Life insurance	$15
Car insurance	$45
Other insurance	$100
Medical bills	NA
Car payment	$250
Credit card debts	$150
Other loans/debts	$100
Savings and retirement	$25
Total	**$2,865**

Mark's Current Monthly Living Expenses

Food	$500
Rent	$1,100
Utilities	$280
Water	$60
Telephone	$110
Transportation	$60
Clothing	$50
Hair care	$60
Hobbies	$70
Dry cleaning	$45
Laundry	$35
Pets	NA
Home decorating	NA
Books and magazines	$5
Gifts	$30
Church and charities	$10
Entertainment	$180
Life insurance	$20
Car insurance	$75
Other insurance	$30
Medical bills	NA
Car payment	$420
Credit card debts	$50
Other loans/debts	$100
Savings and retirement	$25
Total	**$3,315**

Rachel and Mark then calculated their remaining income after expenses.

Rachel	$3,100	Income
	-$2,865	Expenses
	$235	Remaining

Mark	$3,850	Income
	-$3,315	Expenses
	$535	Remaining

Mark and Rachel were surprised at how much extra money slipped away each month. Assuming they had forgotten a few expenses, they decided to count on saving 75 percent of that amount. Therefore, Rachel believed she could save at least $176 a month. Mark could save at least $401. Together, $577 per month could be put aside for the wedding. They needed $4,550 for their share. Rachel and Mark would have to save for eight months to have the money they needed.

Although they planned a wedding date a year away, they wanted to save additional funds to help set up housekeeping. They examined their budgets and found additional ways to save money every month. They then opened an account together, and each agreeing to contribute their promised amounts every month so that they could reach their goal.

Now it's your turn. Go back to your net monthly income. Write that total below:

Bride's monthly income   _____
Bride's monthly expenses - _____
Bride's remaining funds   _____

Groom's monthly income   _____
Groom's monthly expenses - _____
Groom's remaining funds   _____

If you estimate that you can put aside $300 a month for the wedding, and it is ten months away, do not assume that you will have $3,000 for your expenditures. Leave yourself some space for emergencies. Set aside some of that money for unexpected expenses such as illness or major car repairs.

Did the final number disappoint you? You can try cutting back in other ways. Here are a few additional ideas:

- Avoid eating convenience or fast foods, or dining out.
- Cook and freeze ahead as many meals as possible.
- Keep gift giving to a minimum, and explain to friends and family that you are saving for your wedding.
- Plan menus in advance.
- Reduce your clothing purchases.
- Reduce your entertainment budget.

If income and expenses are still too close for comfort, you might have investment assets tucked away that you can use. Here are some possibilities:

Bank savings account
Bonds
Certificates of deposit
Coin or other collections
Jewelry or other valuables
Life insurance, loan or cash value
Money market funds
Mutual funds
Other investments
Real estate
Rental property
Retirement accounts at your place of employment
Stocks

Relying on Monetary Gifts

Should you count on monetary wedding gifts to finance the wedding? In some regions of the United States a large number of wedding gifts are cash. This can create a great temptation for many couples to use money meant for future personal bills to pay for wedding expenses; often they rely on the anticipated income from wedding gifts to pay for those expenses. This can add tension to an already difficult time, causing you to spend your wedding day wondering if your guests have provided enough to keep you going.

Ask around. Is it traditional in your area to receive monetary gifts? Moreover, is it traditional among both of your families? If it is, and you are confident that you will receive an abundance of monetary gifts, it might not hurt to count on a portion in order to have your dream wedding. But keep that portion as low as possible to avoid disappointment and financial distress.

The following is a conservative estimate of monetary gifts. You have invited 200 guests, and in both your families it is the custom to give monetary wedding gifts. You still should not count on more than 40 percent of your guests to give monetary gifts. About 15 percent of your guests won't be able to attend the wedding, or will be unable to give a gift at all. Another 25 percent will give you something more tangible, such as a vase or a vacuum cleaner. Some guests will give you larger monetary gifts than you expected, others will give much less. You should allow a 20 percent discount for those fluctuations.

There are also other mitigating factors. Perhaps you have asked around, and it is customary for guests to contribute $30 per family member as the wedding gift. However, someone with six children probably won't do that. Someone with no children might give you more. It won't necessarily balance out.

If there have been layoffs, job losses, or a large number of weddings recently in either family, your guests' budgets might be extremely tight. In my family we had twelve large weddings in a fourteen-month period. By the time the last wedding rolled around, everyone was broke. I don't think that couple received anywhere near the gifts as the first couple. You may wish to consider this when setting your wedding date.

Last of all, no one ever expects wedding plans to fall apart, but it does happen. I certainly hope it doesn't happen to you. But what if you used all the money that should have been paying personal bills to pay for your wedding and then the wedding didn't happen? You won't receive those gifts you planned to use to pay the rent. Do you want to take that chance?

And in case you are wondering: *It is extremely rude and inappropriate to ask for specific kinds of wedding gifts, such as money.*

Keeping to a Realistic Budget

Rachel and Mark quickly learned that when it comes to planning a wedding, it's easy for things to get out of hand. There are so many items to choose and so many decisions to make It's easy for a couple to simply throw up their hands and forget about their budget. Financial fiascoes occur because it is easy to become overwhelmed by the planning process. That won't happen to you if you observe the following rules:

- Compare prices and services.
- Deal with reputable businesses.
- Keep track of costs on the easy-to-use worksheets.
- Set a bottom-line budget and stick to it.
- Shop carefully.
- Stay organized.

Using the Record and Accounting Diary Worksheets

To organize the information they obtained in one location, Rachel and Mark used the following Record and Accounting Diary worksheets. These helped them keep track of initial estimates, final expenses, deposits, purchases, and other details. A sample portion of the worksheet follows. Refer to this example as you read through the suggested ways to use the worksheets. A series of logs covering all the wedding-related topics follows this sample section so you may track your own expenses. If this is a library or borrowed book, please photocopy the worksheets before you write on them.

Budget 1

Initial Estimate. To determine the price range for the type of wedding they wanted to have, Rachel gathered general information. She talked with friends and family members, made preliminary phone calls, and checked books and magazines. She wrote the general estimated costs in the Initial Estimate column. (See first column.)

Budget 2

Final Estimate. Rachel called caterers, florists, photographers, and other service providers for more specific cost estimates. She asked everyone the same questions so she could compare numbers properly. If she had priced three-dozen roses at one florist and three-dozen daisies at another, she couldn't properly compare the estimates because roses are much more expensive than daisies. Using her more detailed research, she entered the amount she expected to spend for each item in the Final Estimate column. (See second column.)

Budget 3

Target Estimate. Rachel and Mark now had a good idea of exactly what they wanted. They contacted potential service providers and obtained specific estimates, then entered them in the Target Estimate column. (See third column.)

Budget 4

Actual Expense. After comparing prices and services, they hired their service providers, signed the contracts, and placed deposits. Those amounts were entered on the worksheets, in the Actual Expense column. (See fourth column.)

Final Financial Position

Difference. Rachel quickly calculated the variations between the figures in the Actual Expense column and Target Estimate column and entered the discrepancy in the Difference column. "This way we can always determine our financial position at a glance," she told Mark. "The Difference column will show us if we are over or under budget at all times." (See fifth column.)

Here is a more detailed view of the categories on the sample Record and Accounting Diaries. Broad categories such as Stationery are listed by item so you can track the expense for each related item. Typically, all stationary purchased from one source.

For example, Stationery covers several different items that you need to purchase, including:

Announcements

Enclosure cards (reception information)

Invitations

Napkins and souvenirs

Postage

Thank-you cards

Wedding programs

At the end, there is an area to add the totals for each category.

Try to allow an additional 10 percent in your budget for contingencies. If the extra money isn't needed, you will have more available for the honeymoon.

Here is a story example of how Rachel and Mark used the Record and Accounting Diary worksheets to order invitations for 200 people:

After their preliminary investigation, they placed price ranges for their wedding invitations in the Initial column.

Next, they narrowed their choices to two different styles. Based on the prices of those two styles, they listed that range in the Final column.

They then decided on the amount that they expected to spend for invitations and wrote it in the Target Estimate column.

When they ordered the invitations, they listed the cost of the item in the Actual Expense column.

Since the actual cost was $5 less than that in their Target column, they listed -$5 in the Difference column. They were now under budget by $5.

Record and Accounting Diary

ACCOMMODATIONS

Location:

Telephone: **Fax:**

Person to contact:

Date deposit placed: **Amount:**

Balance due: **To be paid on:**

Item	Initial Estimate	Final Estimate	Target Estimate	Actual Expense	Difference
Guest rate					
Miscellaneous					
Total					

Record and Accounting Diary

BEVERAGES

Company:

Telephone: **Fax:**

Person to contact:

Date deposit placed: **Amount:**

Balance due: **To be paid on:**

Item	Initial Estimate	Final Estimate	Target Estimate	Actual Expense	Difference
Champagne					
Beer and wine					
Hard liquor					
Punch					
Drink mix					
Soda pop					
Juice					
Coffee and cream					
Bartenders					
Miscellaneous					
Delivery					
Total					

Record and Accounting Diary

BRIDE'S ATTIRE

Company:

Telephone: *Fax:*

Person to contact:

Date deposit placed: *Amount:*

Balance due: *To be paid on:*

Item	Initial Estimate	Final Estimate	Target Estimate	Actual Expense	Difference
Gown					
Headpiece					
Shoes					
Undergarments					
Jewelry					
Accessories					
Alterations					
Miscellaneous					
Total					

Record and Accounting Diary

CAKE

Company:

Telephone: *Fax:*

Person to contact:

Date deposit placed: *Amount:*

Balance due: *To be paid on:*

Item	Initial Estimate	Final Estimate	Target Estimate	Actual Expense	Difference
Cake					
Decorations					
Cake top					
Delivery and setup					
Miscellaneous					
Total					

Record and Accounting Diary

CEREMONY SITE

Location: _____

Telephone: _____ Fax: _____

Person to contact: _____

Date deposit placed: _____ Amount: _____

Balance due: _____ To be paid on: _____

Item	Initial Estimate	Final Estimate	Target Estimate	Actual Expense	Difference
Rental					
Officiant's fee					
Other Fees/ Gratuities					
Parking					
Decorations					
Furniture					
Setup and cleanup					
Miscellaneous					
Total					

Record and Accounting Diary

FLOWERS

Company:

Telephone: **Fax:**

Person to contact:

Date deposit placed: **Amount:**

Balance due: **To be paid on:**

Item	Initial Estimate	Final Estimate	Target Estimate	Actual Expense	Difference
Bridal bouquet					
Attendants' flowers					
Boutonnieres					
Corsages					
Church decor					
Trellis/Canopy					
Blessed Virgin Mary (Catholic)					
Reception					
Miscellaneous					
Total					

Record and Accounting Diary

FOOD: CATERED

Company:

Telephone: **Fax:**

Person to contact:

Date deposit placed: **Amount:**

Balance due: **To be paid on:**

Item	Initial Estimate	Final Estimate	Target Estimate	Actual Expense	Difference
Catered sit-down meal					
Catered buffet					
Hors d'oeuvres					
Appetizers					
Decorations					
Setup and cleanup					
Miscellaneous					
Total					

Record and Accounting Diary

FOOD: NON-CATERED

Company:

Telephone:　　　　　　　　　　　　**Fax:**

Person to contact:

Date deposit placed:　　　　　　　**Amount:**

Balance due:　　　　　　　　　　　**To be paid on:**

Item	Initial Estimate	Final Estimate	Target Estimate	Actual Expense	Difference
Main dish 1					
Main dish 2					
Main dish 3					
Side dish 1					
Side dish 2					
Side dish 3					
Dessert 1					
Dessert 2					
Dessert 3					
Miscellaneous					
Total					

Record and Accounting Diary

GROOM'S ATTIRE

Company:

Telephone: *Fax:*

Person to contact:

Date deposit placed: *Amount:*

Balance due: *To be paid on:*

Item	Initial Estimate	Final Estimate	Target Estimate	Actual Expense	Difference
Purchase/Rental					
Shoes					
Accessories					
Miscellaneous					
Total					

Record and Accounting Diary

MISCELLANEOUS

Company:

Telephone: *Fax:*

Person to contact:

Date deposit placed: *Amount:*

Balance due: *To be paid on:*

Item	Initial Estimate	Final Estimate	Target Estimate	Actual Expense	Difference
Hair					
Cosmetics					
Gifts					
Ring pillow					
Guest book					
Champagne glasses					
Cake knife					
Newspaper fees					
Other					
Total					

Record and Accounting Diary

MUSIC

Company:

Telephone: **Fax:**

Person to contact:

Date deposit placed: **Amount:**

Balance due: **To be paid on:**

Item	Initial Estimate	Final Estimate	Target Estimate	Actual Expense	Difference
Ceremony					
Ceremony					
Reception					
Reception					
Miscellaneous					
Total					

Record and Accounting Diary

PHOTOGRAPHY

Company:

Telephone: *Fax:*

Person to contact:

Date deposit placed: *Amount:*

Balance due: *To be paid on:*

Item	Initial Estimate	Final Estimate	Target Estimate	Actual Expense	Difference
Engagement photo					
Formal portrait					
Wedding album					
Other locations					
Extra prints					
Miscellaneous					
Total					

Record and Accounting Diary

RECEPTION SITE

Company:

Telephone: **Fax:**

Person to contact:

Date deposit placed: **Amount:**

Balance due: **To be paid on:**

Item	Initial Estimate	Final Estimate	Target Estimate	Actual Expense	Difference
Rental					
Decorations					
Furniture					
Setup and cleanup					
Miscellaneous					
Total					

Record and Accounting Diary

RENTAL ITEMS

Company:

Telephone: *Fax:*

Person to contact:

Date deposit placed: *Amount:*

Balance due: *To be paid on:*

Item	Initial Estimate	Final Estimate	Target Estimate	Actual Expense	Difference
Tables					
Chairs					
Trellis/Canopy					
Dishes and flatware					
Table linens					
Glassware					
Coffee urn					
Serving items					
Podium					
Decorations					
Miscellaneous					
Total					

Record and Accounting Diary

SECURITY

Company:

Telephone: *Fax:*

Person to contact:

Date deposit placed: *Amount:*

Balance due: *To be paid on:*

Item	Initial Estimate	Final Estimate	Target Estimate	Actual Expense	Difference
Ceremony					
Reception					
Overtime					
Miscellaneous					
Total					

Record and Accounting Diary

STATIONERY

Company:

Telephone: **Fax:**

Person to contact:

Date deposit placed: **Amount:**

Balance due: **To be paid on:**

Item	Initial Estimate	Final Estimate	Target Estimate	Actual Expense	Difference
Invitations					
Enclosure cards					
Announcements					
Thank-you notes					
Wedding programs					
Napkins and souvenirs					
Postage					
Miscellaneous					
Total					

Record and Accounting Diary

TRANSPORTATION

Company:

Telephone: *Fax:*

Person to contact:

Date deposit placed: *Amount:*

Balance due: *To be paid on:*

Item	Initial Estimate	Final Estimate	Target Estimate	Actual Expense	Difference
Limousine					
Guest transport					
Other					
Other					
Miscellaneous					
Total					

Record and Accounting Diary

VIDEOGRAPHY

Company:

Telephone: **Fax:**

Person to contact:

Date deposit placed: **Amount:**

Balance due: **To be paid on:**

Item	Initial Estimate	Final Estimate	Target Estimate	Actual Expense	Difference
Ceremony taping					
Reception taping					
Other locations					
Edited tape					
Miscellaneous					
Total					

Record and Accounting Diary

SUMMARY

Item	Initial Estimate	Final Estimate	Target Estimate	Actual Expense	Difference
Accommodations					
Beverages					
Bride's attire					
Cake					
Ceremony Site					
Flowers					
Food: Catered					
Food: Non-Catered					
Groom's attire					
Miscellaneous					
Music					
Photography					
Reception Site					
Rental items					
Security					
Stationery					
Transportation					
Videography					
Total					

Unrealistic expectations and a very real budget can cause tension between you and your fiancé. On the other hand, planning as a couple is a good way to learn about each other's money attitudes. He may like to spend freely, a "live for today" outlook; you might be very nervous if everything is not carefully planned and accounted for. This will be good practice for your future together. You will learn to set goals, compromise, dream, create a plan, and make it happen. If you're like most couples, one of you will be better at organizing, the other at coming up with ideas. It is important that you listen to each other, and learn to work together to create the wedding of your dreams.

Why Get Organized?

The earlier you begin to plan your finances and save money toward your wedding, the easier it will be for you to have the wedding you want. I'm going to tell you about a few other couples' experiences. There is no guarantee of a perfect wedding, no matter how organized. But a little forethought, planning, and an occasional phone call could have saved these couples a lot of grief.

> Cathy assumed that her sister, the maid of honor, was keeping track of the wedding party and their attire. Ten days before the wedding, she went to pick up her dress and asked to see the completed attendants' gowns. The store did not have them. No one had responded to the shopkeepers telephone calls, and the dresses had hung there for eight weeks. According to local law, the shopkeeper was allowed to sell the already paid for dresses to someone else, and she did. Not only did Cathy's attendants have no gowns ready for her wedding, they had paid for gowns they would never own.

> Jim asked his old college buddy to stand up with him at the wedding. Although the buddy was reminded several times to go for a fitting for his formal attire, he never did. The day before the wedding Jim hauled him into the shop; the only available ensemble was three sizes too large, and there wasn't enough time for alterations. His friend looked ridiculous, it detracted from the rest of the wedding party, and in the pictures he makes the whole group look comical.

> Julie's uncle is a minister and because she assumed he would marry her, she never asked. Meanwhile, the uncle agreed to officiate another wedding

that day. A week before the wedding, she not only discovered that she had no one to officiate, she also had a hurt, angry relative to console.

Kevin promised his fiancée that he would handle planning the beverage portion of the evening. He negotiated with various outlets and obtained a large and varied quantity of items at very good prices. He scheduled the delivery, and followed up to ensure that everything was there on the appointed day. However, he not only neglected to hire someone to serve the beverages, he forgot to arrange for glassware!

Heather used spare moments to address the invitations. However, she forgot to cross off thirty-five names that she had completed, and sent those people a second invitation. She then found herself short of invitations and had to pay a large fee to have extras printed and overnight mailed to her so they could be sent out on time.

Planning ahead, will help you avoid major problems and headaches.

The Best Way to Organize

Are you a natural organizer, or do you become tense when you hear any talk of schedules, lists, and worksheets?

For a wedding celebration of any size, it is important to have some kind of a system that will make it much easier for you to have what you want at prices you can afford. All of the helpful information that you obtain for planning and budgeting your wedding will be useless if you don't use it the right way.

Think of this whole endeavor as the equivalent of running a small business. You have to know a little about many different things in order to make the proper decisions. You have to hire people to provide services for you, and budget and coordinate the whole event without letting details slip away.

How do you use your time? How can you change things to your best advantage? Examine your daily life. Try keeping a diary for a week. Either talk into a tape recorder, write a brief note on an index card, in a notebook, or on one of those giant calendars, or set up a computer file. Your entries should be brief, but you should record them often, ideally in fifteen-minute intervals. Record everything, no matter how meaningless.

Did you just spend fifteen minutes trying to find your keys? Twenty minutes waiting in line at the bank? A half hour listening to your friend's problems? Until after the wedding, you should take another look at what such things cost you in time. Concentrate on the essentials during this unique period of your life. Eliminate unnecessary actions that waste your time. Put your keys in the same place every day. Ask the teller when the bank's slow periods are, and try to visit then. Or change banks. If your friend's problems aren't earth-shattering, try and accomplish other tasks while she talks (mend, iron, do your nails, water plants, or start dinner).

You've probably heard that one way to stay organized is to make lists. It's true. Have you ever tried it? Perhaps it didn't work because your mind would go blank whenever you sat down to write the list. Or you successfully made a list, but ended up feeling guilty because you never got all the things accomplished each day. I'm going to help you change that.

First, decide how and where your list will be recorded. It will probably be the same way you kept your daily diary. Use a notebook, a set of index cards, or a computer file. Whatever is easiest and most accessible in your life.

Then start by breaking the place you record your list into three sections:

Do at Once. List the items that are your greatest priorities. These should be the things that will cause you hardship or cost extra money if you don't get them done now. It could be anything from arranging for the reception hall to confirming with service providers or making sure you have your living arrangements set after the wedding.

Important. List things that need to be done soon. That should include things that could be done tomorrow, if necessary, but should be done sometime soon. Anything from picking out your shoes, or selecting music, and working on other decisions that don't need to be made today, but will need to be done soon.

Do When There's Time. List everything that must be done in the next month. These items will slowly work their way up your lists, moving into the Important and then Do at Once lists. But if you keep them on your itinerary, you'll have a general idea of what's coming up and will be less likely to forget about any items.

Complete your Do at Once list daily, and you'll deal with priorities every day. If you have time left, you can tackle the Important list.

Before you go to sleep each night, transfer uncompleted tasks to the next day's list. Consult the list every day, several times a day. You will be surprised what little tasks you can slip in here and there.

There is so much to do in planning a wedding that it is easy to get overwhelmed. Just start somewhere. Break your tasks into smaller steps. Make one phone call, visit one shop, or glance through one book about weddings. Take action and you will feel that you are in control.

Try to pledge an amount of time each day toward planning. Do something every day for at least fifteen minutes. Work up to a half hour or hour. The best way to handle a major project is to take it step by step.

Because it is so important to be organized if you want to save money, here are a few other general tips for organization:

Have one place where everything is kept. It might be a certain desk drawer, computer file, plastic box, or shelf. Put names, estimates, phone numbers, plans, ideas, appointments, and notes from conversations there. If you keep everything in the same location at all times, it will be much easier to find it when you need it.

Give yourself deadlines. Some people shrink from them, but others thrive, and do their best work under pressure. If a deadline gets you moving, set one for each stage of the wedding planning, and meet it.

Delegate. That's what all successful managers do. You probably have done it in many other aspects of your life. Your maid of honor, attendants, mother, sisters, and friends are all possible sources of help. Don't overwhelm any one person with work, but ask each person to gather a little information and do other minor tasks. Be sure to make it very clear exactly what you want them to do, find out, or accomplish.

Be decisive. Many of us have difficulty making decisions, especially when we have too many choices. First, you must gain a general idea of what you want. Then make your decisions and stick with them. The atmosphere and emotions involved with weddings are intensely bizarre. The most decisive and conscientious woman might find herself spending hours debating over the various shades of peach for the hall decorations, or the different writing styles for the invitations.

Perhaps you have tried to follow these suggestions, but still can't organize. Your wedding date is rapidly approaching. It may be time to call in professional help.

Wedding Consultants: Are They Worth the Expense?

If you can't do it yourself, you can hire someone to plan and arrange your entire celebration. A wedding consultant will work with you to choose the right locations and service providers for your celebration. She will also do follow-up work that you might forget.

For example, if you hire a caterer months in advance, there is always a clause in the contract allowing them to increase their prices. Rachel's friend, Katie, was so busy preparing for her big day that she forgot to call and see if there had been a price increase. There was an expensive surprise when she received the bill on her wedding day. Katie told Rachel:

> Originally I planned to invite 150 people. I was quoted a catering price of $26 a plate, which would give me an estimated catering bill of $3,900. Meanwhile, I added thirty guests to my original list, and expected a bill for $4,680. I didn't know that the catering price had increased by $3 a plate. Imagine my surprise when I opened a bill for $5,220. It was $540 more than I anticipated.

If a wedding consultant is doing her job properly, she'll make that call, and quickly inform you about any such changes.

For the most part, you can expect her to deal with reputable services, otherwise she'd be out of business very quickly. She also should be available on your wedding day. It's nice to have someone to keep the show running smoothly so you can relax.

Like all service providers, some are better than others, and all have strengths and weaknesses. You need someone whose outlook matches your own; you must be able to talk freely with her and trust her. She should be skilled in drawing you out and helping you decide what's best for you, and should not urge her ideas on you. If she intimidates you, or doesn't spend enough time answering your questions, or you just don't hit it off, don't hire her.

You must agree on:

- Priorities.
- What services she will provide.
- What fees and charges there will be.
- How often you will be called upon to make decisions.

There are different kinds of consultants (or planners) that assist in arranging weddings. Some do everything from the engagement party to the honeymoon. They make all the telephone calls, obtain and compare estimates, place deposits, and coordinate the activities. You can arrange for a consultant to be available throughout your entire wedding day to keep everything operating smoothly. Some consultants offer their services on an hourly basis. They point you in the right direction by teaching you how to plan and organize. However, you make all of the actual arrangements.

There are many variations between the two. Some consultants specialize in stepping in at the last minute and resolving difficult or tangled arrangements. Others focus their business on arranging traditional formal weddings, or unusual celebrations.

What will it cost? Some are paid a percentage by the service providers that they hire. You only pay a minimal fee. Others charge you a percentage, such as 10 to 15 percent of the cost of all the services they handle. Other planners base their charge on the number of guests. When interviewing, ask in detail about vendor discounts. Some established wedding consultants can obtain so many discounts that the savings they provide actually offsets their fee.

If you are going to hire a consultant, it is essential that you take the time to find one who provides good, reputable service. One problem is that anyone can print business cards and advertise as a wedding consultant. Having a consultant will only save you time and trouble if you find the right one. If you've attended any great weddings, find out if a consultant or planner was used and obtain her or his number. Otherwise, talk to wedding service providers, check your telephone book, and call any listings. When you make your initial calls, have general conversations to see if you're compatible. Ask consultants how long they have been in business, and how many weddings they have handled similar to the kind you want. Ask if they belong to the National Association of Bridal Consultants, which has standards for its members. And always ask for references of recent customers, and call them.

Be sure the consultant understands your budget and is willing to work within it. It won't save you money if your consultant charges more for every item than you would have spent on your own.

Will a consultant be worth the expense? That really depends on you, and on the quality of the consultants available to you. If you are hopelessly disorganized and know that it will be impossible for you or your fiancé to stick to any type of budget, hiring a good consultant might be the best choice.

Service Providers: Getting the Most for Your Money

The best wedding celebration will be a result of skilled professionals doing a good job. Most do, because their business relies on recommendations from previous clients. However, there are some genuine swindlers who make their living by deceiving unsuspecting couples. Before you hire anyone, ask for references and call them. You might also take a moment and call the local Better Business Bureau. You could be surprised to discover a pile of unresolved complaints. Better to know ahead of time than to learn it on your wedding day. Here are seven things you should know before you sign on the dotted line:

Shop around and compare prices. Ask for references, check for quality, and be sure they make it very clear exactly what they are providing for the price quoted you.

It is best if the people you deal with are friendly, personable, and put you at ease. Most people who work in the wedding business are. That shouldn't cause you to hold back any criticisms or complaints. This is still a business transaction. Do not forget that you are their employer.

Have a contract for every service and read it carefully. Make sure that every item provided and its cost are itemized. Question any possible extra charges and tipping policies.

No matter how friendly they are, don't hesitate to ask questions and request agreements in writing. It's good business sense, and they will respect you for that. You are not trying to make new friends; but you are trying to have a wonderful wedding.

Evaluate the service provider's work load. The person or company you are considering rarely returns your calls and is clearly very busy. You assume such popularity means they are very good at what they are doing. Not necessarily. It may be the result of good marketing, or they may be coasting on an old reputation that is no longer valid. Or they might be so busy they would not be able to give you enough time to do a quality job.

Learn the company's cancellation policy. If anything happens and you have to cancel or change the date, you might be slapped with some serious fees. You are signing a contract, and you must honor it.

Don't hesitate to ask questions. It won't cost you a dime. Most service providers will answer freely. If they hesitate, you should too. The more you ask, the more you can compare. And asking questions is the only way you will avoid expensive surprises on your bill.

Remember, you are hiring a professional in order to obtain a quality job. You wouldn't hire a lawn mower mechanic to fix the fuel injectors on your car. Nor should you entrust one of the most important days of your life to a stranger you haven't thoroughly checked out.

Here are are checklists of questions you should ask service providers that could help you save money. (Remember, some things might seem less expensive until you discover their hidden cost.)

CATERING

Company: _____

Telephone: _____ **Fax:** _____

Person to contact: _____

Is your date available?	❑	_____
What menus are available?	❑	_____
At what cost? How is it determined?	❑	_____
What is the serving style? (sit-down, buffet)	❑	_____
What beverages (coffee, tea) are provided?	❑	_____
Is a deposit required? When?	❑	_____
When is the balance due?	❑	_____
Is the rate guaranteed?	❑	_____
Are taxes and tips included?	❑	_____
What is the refund policy?	❑	_____
Are there other events scheduled the same day?	❑	_____
What is the number of guests per server?	❑	_____
Does price include cutting and serving cake?	❑	_____
Are tableware and linens provided? Extra?	❑	_____
Is there a charge for setup and cleanup?	❑	_____
What decoration is provided? At what charge?	❑	_____
What is done with leftovers?	❑	_____

CEREMONY SITE

Location: _____

Telephone: _____ **Fax:** _____

Person to contact: _____

Is your date available?	❑	_____
Is there enough room for your guests?	❑	_____
Is there a charge?	❑	_____
Is a deposit required?	❑	_____
When is the balance due?	❑	_____
Is the rate guaranteed?	❑	_____
What is the refund policy?	❑	_____
What time of day is rental available?	❑	_____
What time of day does rental expire?	❑	_____
Are other events scheduled the same day?	❑	_____
What amount of time are you allotted?	❑	_____
Are musical instruments available? At what cost?	❑	_____
Is a dressing area available?	❑	_____
What is available nearby in case of inclement weather? (For outdoor site)	❑	_____
Is parking available? At what cost?	❑	_____
Is there an extra fee for nonmembers?	❑	_____
Other special regulations or fees?	❑	_____

FLOWERS

Company: _____

Telephone: _____ **Fax:** _____

Person to contact: _____

Is your date available?	❑	_____
Estimated charge:	❑	_____
When is the payment due?	❑	_____
Is the rate guaranteed?	❑	_____
What is the refund policy?	❑	_____
When are they delivered?	❑	_____
How often do they substitute?	❑	_____
Are other events scheduled the same day?	❑	_____
Are there extra decorating charges?	❑	_____
Are rental items available?	❑	_____
Other special fees or delivery charges?	❑	_____

MUSIC

Company: _____

Telephone: _____ **Fax:** _____

Person to contact: _____

Is your date available?	❑	_____
What is the rate? How is it determined?	❑	_____
Is a deposit required?	❑	_____
When is the balance due?	❑	_____
Is the rate guaranteed?	❑	_____
What is the refund policy?	❑	_____
Arrival time?	❑	_____
Number of musicians?	❑	_____
What equipment or instruments are used?	❑	_____
Are other events scheduled the same day?	❑	_____
How much time are we allotted?	❑	_____
Does the price include travel and setup time?	❑	_____
How are partial hours billed?	❑	_____
What are the overtime charges?	❑	_____

PHOTOGRAPHY

Location: _____

Telephone: _____ **Fax:** _____

Person to contact: _____

Is your date available?	❏	_____
Number of weddings photographed?	❏	_____
Will the photographer or an assistant take the photos?	❏	_____
Is a deposit required?	❏	_____
When is the balance due?	❏	_____
Is the rate guaranteed?	❏	_____
What is the refund policy?	❏	_____
Are other events scheduled the same day?	❏	_____
What amount of time are we allotted?	❏	_____
How many locations does this price include?	❏	_____
What are the overtime charges? How are they computed?	❏	_____
Other special fees?	❏	_____
How soon will proofs be ready?	❏	_____
Who selects the final prints from proofs?	❏	_____
When will final prints be ready?	❏	_____
Can we purchase the negatives?	❏	_____
Does photographer's liability insurance cover lost prints?	❏	_____
Does price include completed album?	❏	_____
What is the cost of extra prints?	❏	_____

RECEPTION SITE

Location: _____

Telephone: _____ **Fax:** _____

Person to contact: _____

Is your date and time of day available?	❏	_____
Is there enough room for your guests?	❏	_____
What is the rental charge? Is the rate guaranteed?	❏	_____
Is a deposit required? When is the balance due?	❏	_____
What is the refund policy?	❏	_____
What time of day does rental expire?	❏	_____
Is catering available? At what cost?	❏	_____
Are decorations available? At what cost?	❏	_____
Are table linens, dinnerware, and flatware available? At what cost?	❏	_____
Are beverages available? At what cost?	❏	_____
How are charges for alcohol computed?	❏	_____
Are bartenders available? At what cost?	❏	_____
Is security available? At what cost?	❏	_____
What will the site's insurance cover?	❏	_____
Is parking available? At what cost?	❏	_____
Is valet parking required?	❏	_____
Are tables and chairs available? Extra charge?	❏	_____
Is there a charge for setup and cleanup?	❏	_____
Is there an extra fee for nonmembers?	❏	_____
Special regulations or fees?	❏	_____

VIDEOGRAPHY

Company: _____

Telephone: _____ **Fax:** _____

Person to contact: _____

Is your date available?	❑	_____
Number of previous weddings videotaped?	❑	_____
Will the videographer or an assistant take the photos?	❑	_____
Is a deposit required?	❑	_____
When is the balance due?	❑	_____
Is the rate guaranteed?	❑	_____
What is the refund policy?	❑	_____
Are other events scheduled the same day?	❑	_____
What amount of time are we allotted?	❑	_____
How many locations does this price include?	❑	_____
Are there overtime charges? How are they computed?	❑	_____
Any other special fees?	❑	_____
What kind of equipment will be used?	❑	_____
Are editing and dubbing machines used? Is it included in the price?	❑	_____
How many cameras will be used?	❑	_____
How many camera operators?	❑	_____
Are titles and music included in the price?	❑	_____
How soon wil the tape be ready?	❑	_____
Does videographer's liability insurance cover lost film?	❑	_____
What is the cost of copies?	❑	_____

WEDDING CONSULTANT

Company: _____

Telephone: _____ **Fax:** _____

Person to contact: _____

Is your date available?	❏	_____
How much experience does consultant have with my type of wedding?	❏	_____
Can consultant provide three references from past year?	❏	_____
What is the rate? How is it computed?	❏	_____
Are there possible extra charges?	❏	_____
What are the payment and refund policies?	❏	_____
Other special charges or fees?	❏	_____
Is the consultant bonded?	❏	_____
What are her or his professional affiliations?	❏	_____
What happens if the consultant is unable to complete the planning?	❏	_____

Part Two

SAMPLE WEDDINGS

We've covered the basics. By now you have a pretty good idea of what you can afford, how you will pay for it, and how you would like to spend your money. You've talked to a few service providers, and spent a lot of time discussing the wedding with your fiancé, family, and friends. You've leafed through books and bridal magazines, and thought a lot about your wedding day.

Now it's time to relax a little and see how other couples managed. Here are a few stories, each representing a different type or style of wedding, from which you'll learn some of the methods the couples used to save money while still having themselves a wonderful wedding day.

A Formal Church Ceremony and Indoor Pavillion Reception

Rachel and Mark were married on a brilliant July day at their hometown church. One hundred eighty-five guests attended their ceremony and reception.

On Rachel's wedding day she wore a simple, white silk organza gown. Its scooped neckline set off her shoulders. Woven bands of silk embroidered with crystals and pearls accented the neckline, basque waist, poufed sleeves, and hem. Her headpiece was a pearl and crystal band interwoven with delicate flowers, and a short illusion veil was attached to the back. She paid $780 for her gown, $100 for the headpiece, and $160 for shoes, undergarments, and accessories. She had estimated $800, so she was $240 over budget in this area.

The bridesmaids wore navy satin tea gowns with contrasting white satin scalloped capelets around the bodice and a white satin bows at the waistline. They each carried a picturesque clutch of white stephanotis embellished with pearl and crystal centers and wrapped in white satin ribbons. Each also wore a sprig of stephanotis tied with a tiny pearl-embellished ribbon in their hair.

"Our florist was very helpful in finding ways to save money," Rachel said. "She suggested that for maximum impact we should carry something white and simple. Ribbons add contrast and fullness, yet help keep prices down. I carried a beautiful cascade of white roses, stephanotis, lilies, and Queen Anne's lace. She found a white satin ribbon with pearls and crystals that matched the trim on my dress. My bouquet and the bridesmaids' hair ribbons were made with it. We had attractive arrangements at the ceremony and reception, too. Yet her price was $100 less than we had anticipated."

"We had an elegant and distinctive ceremony," Rachel said. "My cousin Jenny has a beautiful voice, and she has appeared in several area productions. As part of her gift to us, she sang at the ceremony. It was wonderful. I was hoping she would do that, but I hadn't wanted to ask and impose. We paid her accompanist $150 and the organist $75. We had predicted $350 for ceremony music. We saved $125."

"Our photographer did a nice job," Mark said. "We ended up buying more still photos than we had planned, and that was the expensive way to do it. We should have taken the bigger package. The same company sent a videographer, and we have a pleasant and memorable spectrum of the day. We had budgeted $1,000 for those two items, and spent $1,180."

The reception was held at a Winston Park's indoor pavilion, a popular wedding location. Mark said, "The meal was catered on-site, with the rental and catering package all one price, $26 per plate. To hold down our expenses, we trimmed our list to 185 guests. Our total was $4,810, plus additional beverage expenses, which came to $505." Originally, they estimated $4,200 for food and catering, $525 for beverages, and $400 for site rental. The total original allocation for this category was $5,125.

"We spent $5,315, which was $190 more than we planned," Mark continued, "even after trimming the guest list. But part of the additional expense was a change in the menu from our original estimate. We updated the traditional meal by serving blackened redfish in place of fried chicken."

"Our deejay was a treasure." Rachel told me. "He played a great variety of good music all evening and really caught the mood of the crowd. His sound system was superb. And best of all, his charge was $70 less than we had budgeted!"

"Neither of us like the taste of most wedding cakes." Rachel continued. "They seem dry, tasteless, thickly coated with sugary icing, and much too expensive. We rented six round glass cylinders in different heights, and ordered six round cakes from a local deli known for its delicious baked goods. The cakes weren't elaborately decorated, but we were more interested in their flavor. The florist accented the cakes with a small spray on the top of each and garlands of flowers around them on the table. It looked sensational. They tasted delicious, and we received so many compliments. Best of all, we saved $90 from our original estimate of $240 because we simplified the design and had fewer guests."

"We worked hard together," said Mark. "And despite more crises, arguments, temptations, and frustration than I want to remember, we had a great wedding."

"After all the bills were paid, we managed to go only $360 over our original budget. We're pretty happy with that," Rachel concluded.

A Ceremony and Reception at Home

Eric and Tina were married at her parents' home late on a Saturday afternoon in September. Each of them had two attendants, and Eric's niece served as flower girl. Approximately seventy guests attended the ceremony and reception, which was held in the basement of her parents' home.

Tina wore a calf-length, bouffant satin gown with a sweetheart neckline and off-the-shoulder bishop sleeves. A bow topped each sleeve at the shoulder. Delicate beading and lace decorated the bodice to the waist. Her headpiece was a white silk orchid haircomb set in lace that matched her gown, and was accented with streamers of delicate white silk flowers. Eric wore his best gray suit.

The couple used a professional florist, but not for every item. The florist provided garlands of dried flowers, sheaves of wheat, and greenery. These were hung along the living-room walls for the ceremony, and along the basement walls for the reception. The ceremony took place in front of the fireplace, and the mantle held a lovely floral arrangement of roses, carnations, and greenery. The men wore boutonnieres of miniature yellow roses.

Tina splurged on her own bouquet. "I just love orchids, and couldn't imagine getting married with any other flower," she said. "I carried a loose spray of white orchids and maidenhair fern. It was beautiful and worth every penny. That's what we did for the whole affair. Saved money where we could, so we could have the things that were really important to us."

Tina couldn't decide which sister to choose as her maid of honor, so she asked them both. Each wore a simply tailored, knee-length yellow dress with delicate lace at the bodice and sleeves. They found the gowns at a local department store. They each carried a lovely hand bouquet of silk flowers, which they made themselves.

There wasn't much extra room in the basement, so the couple limited decorations for the reception. They selected colorful, delicate lace begonias from a local nursery. Set in planters hand-painted by Eric's mom, they became delightful centerpieces. Tina later planted the begonias around their new home.

The ceremony was followed by a buffet dinner. The couple used the services of a local caterer on a limited basis, purchasing vegetable lasagna and shrimp salad. Tina's mom purchased sandwich items, and fruit, Jell-O, pasta, and potato salads from a local delicatessen. Two neighbors offered to make the coffee and set up the food for the buffet after the ceremony.

Tina rented a large coffeepot, tables, chairs, and a champagne fountain from a local rental outlet. The champagne fountain was the centerpiece for the beverage area, which also included two types of punch (alcoholic and nonalcoholic), soda pop, juice, ice water, iced tea, wine coolers, and beer. They hired a college student to dispense the beverages and prevent the more adventurous youngsters from sampling the alcoholic drinks.

From the local supermarket bakery they purchased a lovely cake, and an assortment of cookies, brownies, and other dessert items for guests to nibble. "The cake was not as big and elaborate as some bakery cakes I've seen," Tina said, "but it was attractive and tasted delicious." Eric's cousin, Ellen, also brought a large plate of her delectable fudge as a contribution to the dessert table.

"We hired a professional photographer who charged by the hour, instead of by the number of pictures we had to buy," Eric said. "We had him there for the ceremony and the early part of the reception, until we cut the cake. He captured the traditional ritual moments. Many relatives took snapshots, and some sent us copies later. We ended up buying almost all the photos the professional photographer offered, but it was still a lot less expensive than some of the quotes we obtained from other professionals. My cousin Jason videotaped the whole event, and presented us with a well-edited two hour tape as his gift to us. He also made copies for other relatives at no charge.

"This was a small, intimate party so a live band was out of the question," Tina said. "But we wanted to have music. We pooled CDs from all our friends and family, and selected our favorites about two weeks before the wedding. Eric's good friend, John, offered to operate the stereo system. We made up a list of the sequence of songs and discs for him to play. For the early part of the evening, we kept the music pretty low key. As the evening went on it became more exuberant, matching the mood of the party."

A Garden Ceremony and Reception

Jeff and Chaundra were married at noon on a Sunday in July. A ceremony and reception with 100 guests took place at separate areas on the grounds of a local park.

Chaundra wore a printed satin gown. The bodice had a beaded appliqué design, and around the V-neck was a delicate lace cape, which draped over her shoulders to form a false capped sleeve. Her headpiece was a white lace bow perched at the back of her head with a waist-length illusion veil edged with the same lace. Jeff wore a dinner jacket, and his attendants wore their best suits. They sported boutonnieres of white tea roses, baby's breath, and violets.

The ceremony took place in a garden arbor. No flowers or additional decorations were needed. The female attendants wore wreaths of baby's breath and ivy interwoven with peach, lavender, and yellow ribbons that matched their tea-length floral gowns. They each carried three white roses tied with lacy violet-colored ribbons. Chaundra's bouquet was of white tea roses interspersed with violets, her favorite flowers.

A student from a nearby music school provided the traditional bridal march and classical songs on a portable keyboard. An a cappella duet from the same school sang several selections chosen by the couple in advance.

The couple hired a professional videographer to tape the wedding ceremony, and ordered an inexpensive photography package from a local professional for the traditional photos. For candid shots, they gave their six attendants disposable cameras, and asked them to record their version of the reception on film.

The reception was a picnic buffet of sliced meats, cheeses, and a relish tray, all purchased from the local supermarket's deli. The food was set on tables borrowed from family members. Disposable tablecloths, decorations, plates, and silverware were purchased from a local discount store. Two teenage neighbors were hired to set up the table decorations, food, and beverages during the ceremony.

Alcoholic beverages were not permitted in the park. The selection of drinks included small bottles of juice and soda pop set in tubs of ice, and large thermos jugs of ice water and iced tea. The guests served themselves.

Each family was asked to bring a cake or nonperishable dessert item. These were displayed on a special table surrounding the "wedding cake." The cake was actually made of three layers of round Styrofoam covered with swirls of creamy white icing. It was decorated with live violets and pansies set in delicate lace. The flowers were surrounded by garlands of peach and yellow ribbons. This was a creative gift from Chaundra's cousin, Jeannette, and it photographed beautifully.

The invitations had specified B.Y.O.C. (Bring Your Own Chair). Guests reclined on a variety of lawn chairs scattered throughout the grounds.

After dinner, a local guitarist entertained the guests with ballads and songs. Jeff and Chaundra had discovered him entertaining the crowd every weekend at a neighborhood restaurant. As the sun was setting over a nearby lake, he ended the evening with a stirring rendition of "The Wedding Song."

Chaundra said, "We also saved money by hand-delivering as many of the thank-you notes as possible at our family reunion. That gathering took place about five weeks after the wedding."

A Hotel Ceremony and Reception

Michael and Colleen were married at a Victorian-era hotel in a nearby resort community. They had seventy-five guests at the ceremony and reception, which was held in the hotel's banquet room.

"By changing our wedding date to mid-September, the hotel's off-season, and scheduling it on a Friday instead of a weekend, we were able to save a third off the regular rate," Michael said.

"We wanted a memorable atmosphere," Colleen said, "and we were able to use the sumptuous surroundings to help keep our budget in line. Having both the ceremony and reception at the same location helps save in many ways. You don't have to worry about arranging transportation, such as taxis, limousines, drivers, and parking attendants. And we saved the extra expense of a ceremony site rental, since there was no charge for having it at the hotel.

"If you plan a hotel wedding, the type of hotel and its location will determine the most cost-effective season and days of the week. In a resort community, weekends and summer days have the most expensive rates. Big city hotels have just the opposite rate schedule. They often offer special weekend packages to attract guests."

"The resort location had extra appeal for our guests," Michael said. "Many came up a few days early, stayed at the hotel at mid-week rates, and then went home on Saturday. Since we had forty-five guests coming up on Wednesday, we chartered a bus to bring them together. My Aunt Grace took care of all the arrangements, and received a free room from the hotel for her trouble."

"Our ceremony was held at 6 P.M. on Friday," Colleen said. "We were married on the hotel's beautiful white front porch. Bountiful baskets of red geraniums and ivy garlands laced with ribbons decorated the pillars and posts. The geraniums were part of the hotel's decor, and they also contributed the garlands as part of the package.

"I wore my mom's wedding dress. It was a beautiful antique satin and lace sheath. I had a matching juliet cap covered with lace, and a short veil. I also wore my grandmother's pearls, and carried the family Bible. Brides have held during their weddings for four generations. It was decorated with handmade lace and yellow roses."

"We each had two attendants," Michael said. "The groomsmen wore dove-gray tuxedos with yellow rose boutonnieres."

"My attendants wore floor-length green satin sheath dresses trimmed with ivory lace. They each carried three yellow roses. We were able to splurge on roses because they were our only floral expense. The background for the location of both the ceremony and reception was already beautifully decorated by the hotel."

"Our biggest expense was the dinner," Michael said. "We never determined the actual cost of the food, because the site rental and everything else was combined into one amount per guest. It came to $55 each, which came to $4,455 for seventy-five guests and a six member wedding party."

"We had a wonderful dinner menu," Colleen said. "It included fresh fruit and two kinds of dip, corn and bacon chowder, marinated green beans, and carrot salad. The entrée was a choice of sweet and sour pork and rice, or prime rib and baked potatoes, and for dessert we chose vanilla ice cream served with brownies. Our guests had a choice of champagne or hot apple cider. Our cake was simple and traditional, and part of the dinner package. It was a marble cake with white icing, decorated with yellow roses. We also saved the cost of servers for the champagne by placing bottles and glasses on every table and having the guests serve themselves."

"Our deejay had a live vocalist who sang to prerecorded music for part of the evening. She was worth every penny of the extra $100 it cost for her services," Michael said. "We learned about her through a desk clerk at the hotel when we asked her about her own wedding. Take a little time to talk to the people who will be making your day special. The chef also went out of his way to produce a special menu, and I think he did it because I spent some time talking to him on the front porch the day we visited the location. I was no longer just a name to him, and that can make a difference.

"Best of all, so many people we care about were able to have a mini-vacation at the resort and be part of our wedding celebration," Michael said.

A Ceremony at City Hall and an Intimate Dinner Reception at a Restaurant

Tim and Jessica were married at city hall on a Friday afternoon in January. His best man, her matron of honor, and fifteen close friends and relatives attended their ceremony and dinner reception.

Jessica wore a beige crepe suit with a fitted jacket and straight skirt with a side slit. The shawl collar, cuffs, and bows were of an elegant satin. In her hair she wore a matching silk headband with a small satin bow. She discovered the gown in the evening-wear section of a local clothing store and made her own headpiece. Dave wore a dark blue blazer and gray slacks.

Jessica carried a small, round bouquet of white roses, stephanotis, and baby's breath. Kari, her matron of honor, wore a corsage of white roses and carnations.

Tim and his best man had white rose and carnation boutonnieres. After the ceremony, everyone joined them for a wedding dinner at a nearby restaurant.

"We wanted to have a nice meal, so we kept the party small," Jessica said. "We were set up in a private room. Guests were served champagne, and their choice of mixed drinks. Our menu included steak, lobster, baked potatoes, and salad. This restaurant is famous for their desserts, so we let our guests choose their own. My cousin, who has a talent for decorating, surprised us with a small cake that turned out beautifully. We had an official cake cutting, and everyone took a piece home."

"We saved money on the rings," Tim added. "We found a diamond wholesaler that was willing to sell to us directly. They even had a selection of settings. We later saw the exact same rings in the mall for three times as much."

"We also made our own gift box," Jessica said. "It cost $35 to rent a fancy box for cards. So I found a medium-sized cardboard box, spent $5 on very fancy wrapping paper and a beautiful bow, cut a slit in the top, and it worked just fine."

A Small Informal Civil Ceremony and Cake-Cutting Reception on a Boat

Scott and Lisa were married at 9 P.M. on the deck of a boat one Sunday in August. They had two attendants and 30 guests present at their celebration.

"I always thought a wedding on a lake would be incredibly romantic," Lisa said. "Then, I saw an ad for a cabin cruiser to rent for an evening, and it really wasn't as expensive as you'd think. The atmosphere was wonderful. It was a beautiful night, although we were pretty nervous about the weather."

While waiting for the sun to set before the ceremony, guests enjoyed champagne or fruit juice and simple hors d'oeuvres. A flutist played simple, haunting melodies that suited the occasion.

"She wasn't a professional musician," said Scott. We just happened to hear her playing while she was sitting in her backyard. It was so beautiful, we asked her to play for our wedding. She'd never performed in public, but after the first few minutes she was fine. We insisted on paying her something, although she said she enjoyed it so much she should be paying us."

The couple were married at sunset by their minister. Lisa wore a calf-length, embroidered organza gown with a dropped waist and full skirt. A delicate collar of lace fell around the bodice, neckline, and capped sleeves. A headband cap of white silk flowers held a small, pouf veil. Scott wore white slacks and a navy blazer.

Garlands of daisies decorated the boat's railing. The cabin reception room had a large floral centerpiece of roses, lilies, stephanotis, and baby's breath surrounded by rich greenery. Lisa carried a cascade bouquet of white lilies, white stephanotis, daisies, and red roses. Her attendants held small sprays of one red rose surrounded by baby's breath and tied with white satin ribbons. Scott and his attendants wore red roses surrounded by baby's breath in their buttonholes. Floral corsages and boutonnieres were also presented to each of their parents and grandparents.

"I'm glad we hired a professional photographer," Lisa said. "We didn't purchase the largest package, but we received fine quality photographs for our album. His pictures of the ceremony at sunset are just fantastic."

The reception took place at the small cabin on the boat. "We had a beautiful cake, made at a bakery," Lisa said. "It was such a small party, the cake was the centerpiece of the food part of the celebration. They did such a beautiful job decorating it that we hated cutting it. We also served coffee, tea, soda pop, and more champagne.

"We wanted the best quality, the nicest things. So we kept the celebration small and we were able to have that," Scott added.

A Formal Church Ceremony and a Small Dinner Reception at a Hotel

Justin and Laura were married at a tiny historic chapel. They each had three attendants, and forty guests were present at the ceremony. A local musician played delicate medleys on her harp both before and during the ceremony.

Laura knew that dresses with a lot of beading and appliqués were the most expensive. She bought a plain, formal princess-style silk organza gown through a retail catalog. She and her mom selected a pattern, then embroidered the satin flowers and sewed on the pearl beading. The pattern was placed on the deep V-necked bodice, sheer bishop sleeves, and repeated in smaller form throughout the skirt and two-foot train. Her grandmother made the headpiece. She created a forehead band from six strands of tiny pearls she had found at a jewelry outlet, and attached two layers of illusion veiling to the back with delicate satin ribbon.

"It turned out to be a beautiful ensemble," Laura said. "It looked like I had paid about six times what I did. However, if a bride wants to do work on her ensemble, she should allow plenty of time. We thought we had. My mom started two months before the wedding. But there are so many other items that need your attention. The last two weeks before the wedding we sewed and sewed. I still see that pattern in my sleep."

She also made her own bridal purse and garter. "I copied a simple drawstring bag style, and made it out of pretty white lace material, lined with synthetic satin," Laura said. "My drawstring was of white satin cord ribbon. For my garter, I covered plain elastic with blue satin, and trimmed it with white lace and a racy red bow. It wasn't that hard, and fortunately I had made those two items not long after I became engaged."

Justin wore a black cutaway tuxedo coat with matching slacks rented from a nearby retailer. He obtained a large discount on his ensemble by having his attendants wear the same style.

The simple, elegant floral arrangements were created with the best flowers for the fall season: gold, cream, and bronze-red chrysanthemums. A tall arrangement stood on each side of the altar. Laura carried a cascading bouquet of chrysanthemums, white roses, and ivy, and her attendants each held a small round version of her bouquet. The groom and male attendants wore boutonnieres of a gold chrysanthemum set in baby's breath. "I checked every florist in the area before I found my best price," Laura said. "It was the last place I called. They did a beautiful job, and were the least expensive in the region."

After the ceremony, the couple strolled down a sunny tree-lined street to the hotel that held their reception. Eighty-five guests joined them in a room decorated with ivy and baby's breath, and splashes of color from button chrysanthemums.

"We found our deejay in the telephone book," Jeff said. "He also had a ceremony videotaping service, and he played a tape at the reception. Part of his package was to offer duplicate videotapes at a large discount to any guest who wanted one. We enjoyed watching the tape while waiting for dinner to be served, and he did a decent job. My uncle took the other photographs at the reception."

The deejay played background music during dinner, and dancing music afterward. "His price was higher than a few others we checked on," Jeff added. "But he did a good job and added to the evening's enjoyment, so he was worth it. Be sure to check references. We were going to hire someone else until we checked, and everyone we talked to was sorry they used him. The deejay we hired received good reports, and I'd give him one too."

The couple had an open bar at their reception, but had arranged to pay by the number of drinks served. Surprisingly, it turned out to be less expensive than the amount they'd budgeted.

"We also saved money by hand-delivering as many invitations as we could," Laura added.

A Formal Church Ceremony and a Large Dinner Reception at a Mansion

Ron and Linda arrived at their historic Episcopal church in an open horse-drawn carriage driven by a liveried coachman. One hundred guests attended their ceremony. The altar was framed with tall planters filled with white roses, lilies, and delicate ferns. Every pew along the aisle was decorated with white ribbons, creamy lace, and dainty pink carnations. A soloist sang selections from Mozart's *Marriage of Figaro*.

Linda wore an ankle-length, medieval-style white poly-silk organza gown. Antique lace and delicate seed pearls decorated the shirred bodice, sleeves, and hem. Her chapel-length veil was capped by a swirl of ribbon rosettes. "I had my gown made by a local seamstress," Linda said. "It was based on a dress in a movie I had seen. The seamstress watched the movie several times, and managed to capture exactly the effect I wanted."

She carried a loose bouquet of white roses, baby's breath, and eucalyptus.

The bride's four attendants wore floor-length pink satin gowns and carried loose arrangements of pink and white carnations and baby's breath. The groom and groomsmen wore white-tie formal wear with tails, and sported jaunty rose boutonnieres. Their ring bearer carried an antique lace pillow, made by Ron's grandmother.

The soloist at the ceremony was a member of the church choir, and the church's organist accompanied her. Both were experienced public performers, yet reasonably priced.

"We shared the cost of the flowers at the ceremony site with a couple who were marrying in the same church later that day," Ron said. "The reception hall was really huge, too big for our crowd, but we loved the historic quality. So we rented plants and a few small trees to decorate the area. They were less expensive than many floral arrangements and took up a lot of space, which gave the room a nice appearance."

The reception was held a few blocks from the church in a historic mansion remodeled for wedding receptions and other large gatherings. Two hundred and fifty guests attended the party. While the bridal party was photographed, the guests went ahead to the reception site and were served champagne.

Thirty-two small tables, each seating eight, were set throughout the room. The centerpiece for each table was hand-dipped white candles with white and pink carnations surrounding the base. The dining centerpiece candles were made by the maid of honor and the other attendants as a special gift to the couple. The white and pink carnations at their base were made of silk. Each member of the wedding party took home a centerpiece as a memento of the day.

Their menu included a variety of salads, a choice of whitefish or pork tenderloin, wild rice, boiled new potatoes, corn, applesauce, and raspberry sorbet. The catering service was part of the rental package at the site. It was a new enterprise, and the couple received an excellent price per serving because the owner felt he would receive plenty of future bookings from their guests if he could make them aware of his services.

A live band played gentle music during the meal and spirited dance tunes throughout the rest of the evening.

The reception had an open bar with a limited selection. The bar closed during the meal and stopped serving alcohol about an hour and a half before the party ended. The bar continued to serve coffee, tea, and soft drinks.

At one side of the hall a three-tier cake stood on display, each layer a different flavor. Linda made her own cake top. "I purchased little bride and groom figurines at a local gift shop, and glued them to a small plastic tier," she explained. "Then I found silk flowers in continuous lengths in pink, white, and gold. I used thin florist's wire to form the flowers into an arch and attached it to the base with masking tape. Then I glued seed pearls, silk flower buds, and delicate leaves around the base, carefully hiding the tape in the process. It looked great—and I received lots of compliments, too!"

Last-Minute Planning: An Informal Wedding

"We're not people who would spend a lot of time planning a wedding." Becky told me. "But that doesn't mean we didn't want a little celebration when we decided to make it happen. Dan proposed on May 25. We didn't have any reason to wait, so we set the date for June 10—enough time to put a little something together.

"I wore a simple white and peach dress, purchased off the rack for $165. My mom made a headpiece to match. She began with a plain straw hat, covered it with white silk and tiny peach flowers, and wove strings of seed pearls and peridot—my birthstone—around the crown. The materials cost approximately $30. My maid of honor Barb wore a pretty flowered sundress and garden hat. Dan and his best man Bob wore slacks and sport coats for the ceremony, and shirtsleeves for the rest of the day.

"My bouquet came from my grandmother's garden. It was a cascading spray of white, lavender and purple lilacs, tied with lace my grandmother gave me. It was very special and stunning, and didn't cost a dime. My maid of honor held a nosegay of carnations and daisies that we bought from a florist. It was very pretty and cost $35. Dan's mom couldn't be there, and my mom didn't want a corsage. So we bought them both pretty music boxes as a memento of the occasion. They were $25 each."

"Barb and her husband Greg have a nice house," Dan said. "We had our ceremony and a champagne barbecue reception in their yard. With only ten guests, we could afford filet mignon for everyone. Greg grilled it, and we had fresh, steamed vegetables from Barb's garden, and a champagne fountain. Dan's sister made a delicious cake, and his brother took the photographs as his gift to us."

Last-Minute Planning: A Formal Wedding

"We talked about getting married," Christina told me. "Then suddenly I was offered a transfer 2,500 miles away. Because David is a writer, he can move with me without harming his income. There was no reason to delay, so we threw together a spring wedding in three weeks!"

"We are good friends with a local judge, and asked her to perform the ceremony," David added. "But we didn't have a location. It only made sense to hold our ceremony and reception at the same place. Chris discovered the local women's club rented their mansion headquarters to nonmembers."

"I couldn't believe it," Christina said. "I always wanted an elegant wedding, and it was a beautiful location that was reasonably priced. We didn't have to decorate. They handled the refreshments as part of the fee. We just arrived, had fun, and left.

"I found my dress in a bridal shop, but I had to purchase the floor sample because there wasn't time to custom order a gown. Because it was discounted I was able to get a nicer dress than I'd hoped. It had a shirred V-necked bodice decorated with scattered pearls, and white silk and pearl roses spilled over the capped sleeves. The gown cost $480. I wore a lace bow with a rose-embroidered illusion veil. It cost $90. If it hadn't cost so much I probably wouldn't have worn it; I felt really strange putting it on. I'm not a hat person, but I did get used to it as the day went on. And it was pretty with my dress.

"My sister Marcie was my matron of honor, and only attendant. She found a pretty pink satin dress that was simple and tasteful, one that she can wear again too!

"I splurged a little on my bouquet. It was a hand-tied arrangement of long-stemmed tulips and white roses, mixed with lilies, eucalyptus, and Queen Anne's lace, held together with white French-wired ribbon. It cost $65. My Aunt Paula has preserved it for me. Marcie wore a wrist corsage of roses surrounding an orchid. It cost $18. We had corsages for both our moms and four boutonnieres. Those all came to $45.

"We had an afternoon high tea reception for thirty guests. Complete with finger sandwiches, scones, biscuits, and assorted petit fours and hors d'oeuvres. We served coffee, tea, punch for the children, and one glass of champagne to all the grown-ups for our toast. We paid the women's club $975 and tipped the three servers $25 each.

"My mom decorated the side tables with votive glasses filled with tiny violets. I love candles, and we must have had twenty burning around the room."

"I have a good stereo," David said. "We collected assorted CDs of soft background music—such as *Celtic Dreams, Distant Hills,* and *Simple Gifts.* My brother kept things operational.

We did hire a professional photographer, and he did a nice job. It cost us $950. As long as we actually look at the pictures once in a while, I can live with that expense."

"I'm glad it worked out this way," Christina concluded. "I had a beautiful wedding, and absolutely no time to get nervous or worried or overwhelmed by millions of decisions. There were few choices available to me on that short notice, but everything fell into place."

No matter what kind of dream wedding you create for your day, there are ways to save money. You've learned quite a few in your reading so far. The next section will give you several hundred additional cost-saving ideas. Search first for ideas through the categories listed alphabetically that represent the largest part of your budget. Then look through the categories that are your lowest priorities. You'll find great ideas in all the sections—and remember, money does not necessarily buy quality or elegance.

Part Three

MONEY-SAVING IDEAS

Accessories

- Purchase a style of shoes that you will use as dress shoes later on.
- Buy simply styled shoes on sale to match your dress.
- Borrow shoes from a recent bride and have them dyed to match your gown (with her permission).
- Wear plain ballet slippers; they are often comfortable and much less expensive than formal shoes. If you have a floor-length gown, who will see them?
- Look for beautifully decorated ballet slippers in the lingerie department or in catalogs. They are an inexpensive alternative if your wedding will be indoors.
- Borrow a slip, have it made by a seamstress, rent one, make your own, or buy it at a department store, factory outlet, or discount outlet. Go anyplace but a bridal shop—they are most expensive there.
- Borrow a bridal purse.
- Make your own bridal purse. Find a pattern for a simple drawstring bag. Purchase pretty material the same color as your dress. Stitch it together and use a ribbon for the drawstring.
- Cover elastic with satin fabric, trim with lace, add a pretty bow, and you have your own garter!
- Make your own ring bearer's pillow. You'll find all the materials at any fabric shop.
- Obtain a free makeover at a cosmetic studio about one month before the wedding. If you like it, have them do your wedding-day cosmetic application.

Attendants

- Reduce the size of your wedding party, and you'll save on flowers, gifts, and transportation.
- Save on lodging and transportation by asking local people to be your attendants. Lodging, transportation, and entertainment for attendants from out of town can be expensive.

- Have your bridesmaids' luncheon at home. Make a tray of sliced vegetables and cold cuts, or have one prepared at a deli, and pick up a few salads and dessert.

- Attendants' gifts are just supposed to be mementos to remind them of your wedding day. They don't have to be expensive.

- Make your attendants' gifts—they'll treasure them even more.

Beverages

- Don't serve the cocktails before dinner.

- Serve low-salt snacks during the cocktail hour, people will drink less.

- Purchase wine by the gallon, and beer by the keg. A keg of beer contains about 15 gallons.

- Buy correct quantities to eliminate leftovers. For 100 people allow 24 quarts of soda pop, 2½ pounds of coffee, ½ pound of tea, 3 quarts of cream, and 2½ pounds of sugar. If you are providing a larger variety of beverages, you can reduce these quantities.

- Assume one glass of champagne per adult guest. A 26-ounce bottle will yield eight servings. The yield will be the same for wine; but if it is served through the bar a greater quantity will be used.

- Hard liquor at most receptions includes whisky and vodka. A 64-ounce bottle will yield about sixty-four drinks. If you serve shots during the toasts, compute an additional amount for those.

- Use "house brand" liquor as opposed to name brands.

- If you plan to serve mixed drinks, allow one part liquor to three parts mix such as soda, cola, and orange juice.

- Adding champagne to the punch will cost about $1.50 per person.

- Use a sparkling wine or cider instead of champagne.

- An open bar costs about $3.50 to $5 per person for each hour of the reception.

- Sometimes it's less expensive to be billed per drink, rather than per person. Find out if the charge is based on the number of adults attending the wedding or the number who actually drink alcoholic beverages. It can make a big difference in your quoted price.

- Provide a limited variety of alcoholic beverages at the reception by serving only beer, wine, and punch.

- Some establishments allow you to bring your own alcoholic beverages (purchased elsewhere), but they charge cork fees for every bottle opened. Sometimes the fee is so expensive you don't save money bringing your own beverages.

- Line up small bottles of juice, sodas, wine coolers, beer, and bottled water at the end of the buffet table in place of a bar. Have glasses nearby, or placed on the dining tables.

- Buy alcoholic beverages from a wholesaler if it's legal in your state.

- Purchase beverages from a dealer that will give refunds on unopened bottles. Some states however, have laws against this.

- Encourage bartenders to serve standard shots, not doubles.

- Close down the bar and serve coffee one hour before the party ends.

Cake

- Bake your own wedding cake. You can write to the company for directions if you use a package mix.

- Ask a friend or relative to bake and decorate the cake.

- Serve only cake and punch after the ceremony.

- Cake producers base their charge on the number of servings, or on the number of slices you will need. Don't order a bigger cake than you will use.

- Have friends and relatives bring cakes. If you want a more picturesque cake for your photo album, have someone frost and decorate Styrofoam. That's what bakers do for their shop windows.

- Bake your own sheet cakes ahead of time and freeze them.

- Supermarket bakeries are often less expensive than other bakeries. But their decorating may be less detailed.

- Have the bakery make and decorate a small wedding cake. Use it for pictures, and have it served to the parents and bridal party. Make your own sheet cakes for serving the guests (these cakes should be in the kitchen waiting to be sliced while you cut the small cake).

- Instead of paying the caterer for dessert, ask friends to bring treats for a sweet table.

- Use your wedding cake as the dessert, instead of sending it home with the guests.

- If you wish to have a fountain cake or additional items such as bridges and steps, then allow for significant cost increases.

- Make your own cake top.

Catering

- Have your meal catered through your supermarket deli if it will be a small, informal gathering. This can be a quarter the cost of a regular caterer.

- Find out if the taxes and tips have been included in an estimate, and how they were computed so that you can properly compare costs. Some caterers include tax and tips in their fee quote, others don't.

- Know if the quoted cost per plate from your caterer includes charges for tableware and food servers. If it does, find out the amount of tableware and number of servers so you can properly compare estimates.

- Cook part of the meal and have the rest catered.

- Hire your own food servers rather than using a catering service.

- If the reception is at a church hall, they may have their own kitchen crew that will cater your party at a lower cost than a professional catering service.

- Order the minimum menu from any caterer. Avoid fancy extras.

- When you sign a contract with a caterer, especially far in advance of your date, make sure there is a cap on price increases.

- If you hire a caterer, labor costs are a large portion of your bill. The more complicated the dishes on your menu are, the more you will pay in labor costs.

- Having your meal served buffet style is not necessarily the least expensive way. If you offer a larger variety of foods over a longer period of time, it may cost you more.

- Negotiate a discount or special cost per plate for children's meals if you will have very many children at the reception meal. Some food providers will agree to this, because children consume much smaller portions.

Ceremony Site

- Ask if there is a charge to use the site. If there is, what services are provided for that fee?
- If you are not a member of the church in which you will marry, ask if they charge an extra fee for nonmembers.
- Alternative sites—homes, gardens, historic mansions and sites, art galleries, nature centers, and many other public sites—are often less expensive. But they are not always set up for weddings, so there may be extra work setting up and cleaning up the site.
- Ask about decorations if you are planning a wedding during a holiday season, such as Christmas or Easter. A church may already have lots of decorations. However, some Christian denominations discourage weddings during Advent and Lent. Jewish synagogues also discourage weddings during certain fast days and festivals.

Decorations

- Do your own decorating at the reception site. Try to get access the day before the wedding.
- If the background site is pretty, don't bother with decorations.
- Make your own decorations. Craft books at the library offer ideas and directions.
- Rent, buy, or make a money box. Renting or buying a money box costs $20 to $50. To make one, wrap a large empty gift box with beautiful paper and bows, and make a slit in the top.

Flowers

- Ask florists if they charge a consulting fee before you meet with them. Most don't, but some use this as a way to add to their profits. You want to know about it before you've met with them.
- Ask if there's a delivery and setup charge when you compare prices among florists. Some florists sound less expensive, until they sock you with these charges at the end.
- Plant and grow your own flower garden, and make your arrangements yourself. However, this requires a great deal of time, and you shouldn't attempt it if you're having a large wedding.

- Purchase flowers in bulk from a nursery and arrange them yourself.
- Check under Florists in the yellow pages for a wholesale flower market near you that sells to the public. If you can't buy direct yourself, see if a local florist will purchase them for you for a small fee. (However, you must do the transporting and arranging yourself.)
- Buy silk flowers and arrange them yourself. They can be expensive, so keep your eye on prices.
- Use the most popular and inexpensive flowers of the season. In spring use: anemones, daffodils, tulips, forsythia, heather, and apple blossoms. From summer through fall use: baby's breath, carnations, daisies, gladiolas, lilies, roses, and stephanotis. In winter use: amaryllis, carnations, and chrysanthemums.
- Choose simple designs or single-stemmed flowers. Fifty percent of the florist's charges can be labor.
- Carnations, daisies, baby's breath, ivy, eucalyptus, chamomile, September wheat, and ribbons are inexpensive items that add fullness to your bouquets and arrangements.
- Try not to get married around Easter, Mother's Day, Valentine's Day, or during prom season. Flowers cost more at these times and florists are also extremely busy.
- Prominently feature your more expensive flowers, and save money by minimizing the quantity.
- Minimize the number of flowers in each arrangement. You can fill out arrangements and add depth by using smaller, less expensive flowers (such as mini carnations) deeper down in the bunch.
- Use a combination of fresh and dried flowers in your arrangements.
- Instead of a bouquet, carry a floral covered prayer book, with satin ribbon streamers.
- Carry a simple nosegay in place of a large, cascading bouquet.
- You and your attendants could each carry a single flower.
- You and your attendants can carry wildflowers.
- Have your attendants carry a bouquet of baby's breath tied with brightly colored ribbons.
- Ask if anyone else is marrying at your site on the same day. Contact them and see if they'd like to share the costs of decorations.

- Color is as important as size when it comes to altar arrangements. Use flowers of one color, such as white, to give the illusion of substance and opulence.
- If you are having a church wedding, decorate the aisle and pews with ribbons and lace instead of flowers.
- Decorate every other pew row, or just the first few rows where the attendants and immediate family will be seated if you marry in church.
- Arrange for the ceremony flowers to be transferred to the reception site if your ceremony site is not a church.
- Use potted plants and flowers at the ceremony and reception sites that you can later use to decorate your home.
- Rent plants and small trees for background arrangements. Some local nurseries will rent these for a minimal charge.
- Make your own decorative background garlands. Measure the area (string is helpful) and use pine boughs, dried straw, wheat sheaves—whatever works. Wire them together in small bunches and attach to a long thin wire. Add fresh flowers here and there if you want, but use sturdy types that don't require much water. Mist the garland to keep it fresh.
- Add a rich, elegant look to a simple white centerpiece by spraying the green leaves with gold metallic paint.
- Use flowering plants as table centerpieces.
- Use single flowers in bud vases as centerpieces for the reception tables.
- Forego a going-away corsage if you and the groom are sharing expenses.

Food

- If you have a morning wedding, you can have a wedding breakfast.
- Offer a cold lunch buffet—slices of meat and cheese, a relish tray, salads, and cake.
- Have a simple reception of punch and hors d'oeuvres in the afternoon.
- Have your reception begin and end well before the dinner hour, or much later. However, your guests should be aware that they won't receive a meal.
- Cook your own meal, and serve it buffet style.
- If you plan to provide food for your musicians, photographers, and other service providers at the wedding, serve them sandwiches and nonalcoholic beverages. They do not need to eat the same meal as your guests.

- Use ready-made food for your meal.
- Ask each family to bring a dish. Someone must coordinate the menu, but you need only provide the plates, utensils, napkins, cups, beverages, etc.
- Purchase entrées directly from a caterer. Ask guests (or immediate family and friends) to bring the side dishes.
- Purchase food from wholesale suppliers that sell to restaurants. If they will sell to you directly, you can obtain large quantities at a sizeable discount.
- Try to purchase the correct quantities to avoid leftover waste. To feed 100 people, use 38 pounds of ham, beef, veal, or pork, 31 pounds of potatoes, 7 pounds of rice, 25 pounds of vegetables, and 15 heads of lettuce. Allow each person two pieces of chicken. Reduce the quantity if you are serving more than one kind of meat. The more side dishes you provide, the more you can reduce the quantity of your main dishes.
- Borrow items that you normally would rent, such as a coffeepot, punch bowl, tables, and chairs.
- Set your own tables.

Formal Attire

- Remember that the proper fit of the garment can be more important than the price.
- Choose a shop that has a reputation for quality care and professional service.

Gown

- Ask your mother, aunts, grandmothers, sisters, and cousins if they know of any gowns in storage. There may be some beautiful gowns packed away in family attics.
- If you attend a bridal fair, be wary of gowns that are called discontinued or overstocked. You have a cash-and-carry deal here, nothing is returnable and there is no custom fit.
- Be sure you ask about refund policies when you buy your dress. You may find the perfect dress elsewhere a week from now, or have to cancel for some other reason. In some shops, the minute you walk out the door, cancellation means you forfeit the deposit, or pay for the gown anyway.

- The cost of your dress will depend on its intricacy of style, material, amount of trim work, value, and number of alterations made to the original design.
- To help avoid making emotional decisions when you try on dresses, tell shopkeepers your budget, and ask that they only show gowns in that price range.
- Take your time shopping, so you don't get caught up in the emotion of the moment. Most clerks work on commission. No matter what they say, remember, they are there to sell you a dress and will praise whatever they think you'll take.
- Buy a gown off the rack in a department store, especially if you're planning to wear a tea-length dress and aren't particularly attached to wearing white.
- Order a bridesmaid's gown in white, and use it as your wedding dress.
- Wear an evening gown or prom dress for an informal wedding.
- Buy a secondhand dress through a resale shop or newspaper advertisement. Think of all the beautiful gowns that were worn only once. And since there isn't a huge market for secondhand gowns, you may be able to find one at a bargain price.
- Look in the classified ads for expensive, beautiful gowns that were never worn. You could find a $1,000 dress offered for $300—and an owner willing to take even less to get it out of her life. Of course, it should fit, or need only minor alterations.
- Rent a gown. Check local outlets for details.
- Buy a sample gown, the one customers try on to see dress styles.
- Ask about discontinued lines. Fashions and fabrics change each year, and many are sold at a great discount at the end of the season. Sometimes a manufacturer will stop producing a beautiful dress because it's no longer profitable to make.
- Some shops mark down their entire lines after the season. Make sure the fabric is suitable for the season of your wedding.
- Discount Bridal Service consultants can sometimes obtain designer gowns at reduced prices.
- Several large department store chains offer wedding gowns, headpieces, and attendants' and flower girls' dresses in their catalogs. The prices are very reasonable, and if you order early you ensure obtaining everyone's proper size.

- JCPenney now has a bridal catalog. The prices are reasonable, and the items arrive very quickly.
- Sew your own dress or have it made. There are many patterns available, or you can select a gown you love and have it reproduced in a less expensive fabric.
- Shop around at a number of fabric shops. Fabric and materials might be on sale.
- Glued on beads or pearls are much less expensive than those that are sewn on.
- If you'd like to make your own dress but are afraid of ruining expensive fabric, purchase inexpensive material to try out the pattern first.
- Avoid real silk if you are sewing your own dress. It is the hardest fabric to work with. Use synthetic silk or other fabrics.
- Synthetic fabrics are less expensive.
- Obtain a written estimate of alteration charges before placing your order. Some shops make a big profit on extensive and expensive alterations.
- For alterations some shops charge a flat fee, others a fee for each item. Common wedding dress alterations are taking in or letting out the waist, bodice, shoulders, or side seams; shortening sleeves or hem; and adding beadwork. Alterations can add $50 to $500 to the price of the dress.
- Ask what size is ordered. Some shops purposely order a larger size so that you will have to pay for expensive alterations.
- Make sure there are no hidden charges, like for "pressing" the gown.

Guest List

- Every guest adds to the cost of invitations, thank-you notes, postage for both, and refreshments.
- Cut your reception guest list by inviting most of your local guests to the ceremony only. But be very clear so that you avoid confusion. A formal invitation for the ceremony is not necessary if it's a smaller wedding. Just contact guests by phone or in person.
- Out-of-town guests should be invited to both the ceremony and the reception, or they should receive an announcement only.
- If you hold a reception at a hotel, ask if it will offer a discount for your guests' rooms.

Headpiece

- Check the closets of family members. If the owner agrees, a headpiece can be adapted or changed to match the dress. Or remove the veiling, and attach it to a cap piece you've selected.

- Buy illusion veiling material in a fabric shop and make your own headpiece. Attach veiling to a simple wreath or cap piece. You can decorate it with flowers, bows, lace, beads, and pearls if you like. Decorated caps and headbands are often available in fabric shops.

- Buy a never-used or secondhand veil through a resale shop or newspaper advertisement.

- Look for sale, discounted, closeout, and discontinued items at bridal shops or department stores.

- Wear flowers or a decorative comb in your hair in place of a traditional headpiece.

- Have it made by a seamstress.

Honeymoon

- Travel in the off-season. Rates to popular destinations such as Florida or the Bahamas can be much lower in the summer. Find out the date when the rates change and plan accordingly.

- Camp at a state or national park near your home.

- Stay one or two nights in a bridal suite.

- If you have a hotel reception, you may be able to get their bridal suite free, or at a big discount.

- If you'll be traveling by car, save money spent on lunches by packing a cooler with lunch meat, soft drinks, fruit, and other picnic items.

- Ask about special package plans or honeymoon rates when you call to make reservations.

- Join a package tour to your honeymoon location.

- Have a combination honeymoon: camp out some nights, stay in hotels others.

- If you stay in hotels, pick up bakery items for breakfast, and eat them in your room.

- Check hotel regulations; some don't mind if you bring along a hot plate. You can use it to make tea, coffee, or soup in your room.

- If you find yourself out priced by the restaurant at your honeymoon spot, ask employees where they eat. It's often much cheaper.

- Ask the restaurant to fill your thermos with hot coffee before you retire to your room in the evening. It will be waiting when you wake up in the morning.

- Carry a flask of your favorite liquor. You can make yourselves predinner drinks in your room.

- Economize on meals by eating at fast-food restaurants some days, then you'll have the money to splurge on a few expensive dinners.

- In some areas, hotels and motels in the state park will be less expensive than those on the outside. Check and see if that applies to the area you're visiting. Make reservations early—these places are often booked far in advance.

- Stay at bed-and-breakfasts.

Invitations

- Purchase invitations through mail-order catalogs, often mentioned in bridal magazines. They are of good quality, and generally less expensive.

- Send photo invitations or thank-you notes. These can double as keepsake souvenirs.

- Ceremony programs are not expensive, but if your budget is tight they can easily be eliminated.

- Hand deliver invitations and thank-you notes to people you often see. It will save postage.

- Don't put a postage stamp on the reply card envelope. It has never been an etiquette requirement, but has become a customary way to give invitees an incentive to return the response cards.

- Make sure you order enough invitations. In so many weddings, a few additional invitations are needed at the last minute. It's much more expensive to order a few additional invitations after your initial order has been processed.

Music

- Ask a friend or relative to play the musical accompaniment.
- When selecting a ceremony site at a church or synagogue find out if the "house" musician gets a token fee whether they're used or not. If they do, it may be best to use them.
- Ask a talented friend or relative to sing.
- Try to bargain with the musicians, perhaps offering $50 or $100 less than their asking price.
- Use music you've taped yourself.
- Have one classical guitarist or pianist rather than a string quartet for dinner or background music.
- Hire a deejay.
- Hire a local vocalist who isn't a professional, and you will pay a smaller fee. Check church choirs and the music departments of nearby high schools and colleges. Make sure your performers have some experience in public or they may panic at the last moment.
- Have a live vocalist sing to recorded music.
- Some halls have background music that can be piped in during the dinner hour.
- Hire a live band for the early part of the evening, and use prerecorded music for the rest of the night.

Photography and Videography

- Have your bridal portrait done at home on your wedding day to save the studio fee. (Be sure to allow enough time for this.)
- Use a professional photographer's smallest package. Offer to supply film to a few friends and ask them to take candid pictures throughout the day.
- Ask a friend to take all the wedding pictures. Rent a camera if he or she doesn't have a good one.
- Purchase ten or fifteen disposable cameras and distribute them among trusted friends or relatives. Ask them to snap candid shots throughout the evening, and assign someone to collect them at the end of the night.
- Shop around for photographers. A good photographer who is trying to establish business might be much cheaper than a well-known pro.

- Some photographers now charge by the hour instead of by a minimum number of photos you must buy.
- Rent a video camera or ask someone you know who owns a video camera to record the day.
- Have a videotape of the ceremony only.

Reception Site

- Do your own setup and cleanup at the hall.
- Reserve facilities early. The least expensive places go first.
- Find out if there are overtime charges for the hall, how much they are, and how they are computed.
- When you are comparing reception sites, remember that some include the hall rental with the catering price, and others don't. You need to know this so you can compare prices.
- Read the hall contract carefully. Some sound less expensive until they nickel-and-dime you with additional charges.
- If reception site has piano or taped music available, ask if there is a charge for use.
- A reception dinner in a restaurant banquet room is less expensive if you're not planning a big formal bash or to have music.
- Find out if there are additional charges for use of the cloak room, security and parking attendants, doormen, or maintenance workers.
- Pick a place where the deposit is refundable, or at least a portion of it is.
- Reception halls are often less expensive in the least popular wedding months—late January, February, March, and November.
- You'll pay highest rates and have the most trouble finding services on the most popular wedding dates—the Saturdays in May, June, September and October.
- Have your reception at a private home, nearby clubhouse, or outdoor park, or rent a hall (church, lodge, or sorority) or historic home.
- Have your wedding and reception at home.
- If you are having a home wedding, have a clean up–fix up party a few weeks before your wedding date. Invite the wedding party. They'll get to know each other and you'll get the house spruced up. Serve refreshments.

- Your estimate of the attendance at the reception that you give the caterer is very important. If you must pay for the number of guests listed on the contract—or guarantee a minimum number of guests—it could be a heavy cost overrun if you estimate incorrectly.

Rings

- Purchase your rings from a reputable wholesaler.
- Buy them at a pawn shop—but have a qualified appraiser examine them first.
- Many coin shops deal in jewelry and sell pieces for the gold content value only, which is often much cheaper than buying from a jeweler.
- Check to see if there are any family heirlooms that could be used as a setting.
- See if divorced relatives will sell you their rings.
- Avoid shopping at a mall jewelry store. Their merchandise will be overpriced.
- Stones from other pieces of jewelry can be mounted in a ring setting.

Service Providers

- Reserve services early. The least expensive caterers, florists, and photographers are usually booked first.
- Hire good security. Couples have been robbed after leaving their reception in their wedding finery with all their monetary gifts.
- If you buy special money envelopes individually for the vocalist, minister, and other service providers, they can cost $1.50 each. Buy them at many card shops in packages of ten for $2.50.
- Use credit cards such as Visa or MasterCard to pay for as many items and services as possible. This gives you the additional coverage of a consumer protection law. If you have a problem with the quality of goods or services that you haven't been able to resolve on your own, contact your credit card company. It's possible that you won't have to pay the bill for it. But you must contact the original company to settle the dispute first. If that doesn't work, contact the credit card company promptly. Don't just ignore the payment. You need their permission, or not paying the bill can harm your credit record. (Note: This applies only to purchases over $50, and must be

a purchase made in your home state, or within 100 miles of your mailing address at the time.)

Setting the Date

- Peak wedding seasons vary by region. In many regions, spring and fall are peak wedding times, so it's best to marry in summer or winter. But in many areas of the South and Southwest, winter months (especially February) are extremely popular wedding months.
- The busiest times are Saturdays in May, June, September and October. At these times it will be hard to find any sites, and discounts will be scarce.
- Saturday is the most popular day; choose Friday or Sunday instead.
- Get married on a weekday. Sites and services may be cheaper. However, it may be more difficult for your guests to attend.

Transportation

- Borrow cars from friends and family, rather than renting limousines.
- Ask a travel agent about discounts and special plans for your honeymoon.

Two Things You Should Not Do to Save Money

- Have a cash bar at the reception.
- Have a dinner where your guests pay for their own meals.

Other Wedding Books by Pamela A. Piljac

THE BRIDE'S THANK-YOU GUIDE

Thank-You Writing Made Easy

Makes writing memorable notes both easy and fun by answering etiquette questions and providing more than 60 sample letters.

ISBN 1-55652-200-2
96 pages, paper, $5.95

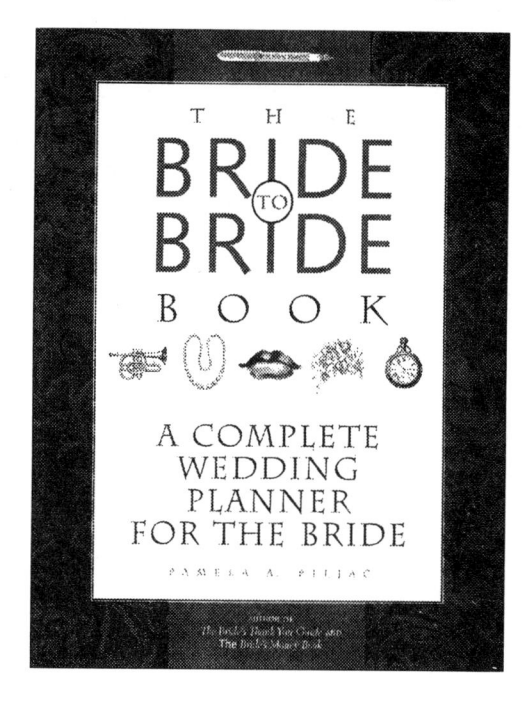

THE BRIDE-TO-BRIDE BOOK

*A Complete Wedding Planner for the Bride
Revised Edition*

Here is information for the busy bride of the nineties, in the revised edition of a book that has sold over 85,000 copies.

ISBN 1-55652-270-3
160 pages, paper, $11.95

These books are available through your local bookstore or directly from Independent Publishers Group, 814 N. Franklin Street, Chicago, Illinois, 60610, 1-800-888-4741. Visa and MasterCard accepted.